G000257722

Machine Knitting

A Practical Guide

Also by Jane Anthony

The Story of Foal Farm
Wistaria Street Will Soon be Gone
The Young Stranger
Our Patients Never Say a Word
The Emergency Book

MACHINE KNITTING

A Practical Guide

Jane Anthony

('Sally' of *WOOLGATHERING* — formerly in *MODERN KNITTING*)

MACDONALD AND JANE'S • LONDON

First published in Great Britain in 1977 by
Macdonald and Jane's Publishers Limited
Paulton House
8 Shepherdess Walk
London N1 7LW

Reprinted 1977

ISBN 0 354 04137 1

*Printed and bound in Great Britain by
Redwood Burn Limited
Trowbridge & Esher*

Contents

Acknowledgments and Thanks

I thank every firm or individual mentioned in this book: they have all given enthusiastic help. In fact, so many people have been so kind that it is hard to pick out just a few, but I must say a special 'thank you' to *Knitmaster Limited:* my years of happy association with this firm — the freedom to walk around and talk to their knitters and designers, and the wonderful letters I received from readers of their magazine (who know me as 'Sally' of 'Woolgathering') — have taught me more about machine knitting and its endless possibilities than I could otherwise have learned. Mr. Rolly Groom and Mr. Sim Groom were outstandingly kind and generous; Miss Jean Wiseman (Press Officer) was unfailingly helpful; and although I cannot name them all, I wish to say that everyone on the staff, both at Battersea and at Chiltern Street, gave me a friendly welcome and every possible help.

Special thanks, too, to two knitting friends: Mary Weaver (of Weaverknits); I have spent so many happy hours talking knitting with Mary that I only hope I haven't quoted her actual words too often (though I am sure she will forgive me if I have) and Alice Burkhard (of Alice's Knitting and Crafts Centre) who taught me a lot in my early days.

All these people — and many more — have added to the fun and pleasure of machine knitting, and given me the confidence to write this book, which I hope will help other knitters to enjoy their machines as much as I enjoy mine.

Picture Acknowledgements

I wish to thank:-

Jones Sewing Machine Co for the use of the pictures on pages 52, 68 and 74. (these garments were designed and made by knitters who had just completed their postal tuition)

Knitmaster Limited for the use of the pictures on pages 11, 31, 47, 96,

125 and for the diagrams on pages 12, 49, 53 and 55
Metropolitan Sewing Machine Company and Harry Taylor for the use of the pictures on pages 6 and 104
Metropolitan Sewing Machine Company and Norman Perry for the use of the pictures on pages 58 and 117 (these were taken at their charity fashion show during autumn 1976 — all garments made, and many of them designed, by members of their knitting club)
Passap Limited for the use of the pictures on pages 28, 80 and 131

Note:

Every knitting machine should have its own instruction book, written especially for that machine, and in my view RULE NUMBER ONE, in machine knitting, is to study that book until you clearly understand the working of your machine.

Your instruction book is a vital part of your machine; you have paid for it, just as you have paid for the needle bed and the carriage and all the other parts of your knitter, and this book is NOT meant to take its place, but to show knitters that learning the mechanics of the machine is only the beginning of the adventure.

After that comes the saving (and earning if you wish), the pleasure of having more (and better) clothes for less money than you used to spend, and the thrill of creating beautiful things, out of your own mind, by way of your own knitting machine.

I realise that some older machines had instructions that need a little puzzling over, and that some knitters may have bought second hand machines without instructions. I have given what help I can, on this point, in Chapter Two.

Important

The United Kingdom addresses of many firms, journals and individuals referred to in the text are listed in the Appendix on page 133. Readers in countries other than the United Kingdom who wish to contact any of those so listed should check whether there is a representative in their own country. In any case of difficulty, write to the United Kingdom address for advice or help.

Why I am Writing This Book

I bought my first knitting machine in 1961, and quickly became fascinated with it. Within a short time I was making beautiful woollies for family and friends, for about a third of the shop price.

I was thoroughly enjoying it, too. I lead a busy life (I am a full time writer, with a home to run) but so far I had lacked the pleasure of making things with my hands, and machine knitting filled the gap delightfully. I often knitted when I ought to have been doing something else — and this was at a time when my life was very happy and pleasant.

The following year things changed. As a matter of conscience (and with my full agreement) my husband took a job that drastically altered our living conditions and brought great strain. And machine knitting was no longer just an enjoyable hobby — it was a lifeline. I would never have got through those five hard years without it. Whenever I was 'down', a knitting session relaxed and cheered me.

When the bad patch was over, I was as keen as ever. I began to be interested in other machines (my first was a Passap Duomatic). I bought a secondhand Passap Automatic (for £15, and it was good value). When the Jones Lacemaker came out, I bought one and sold my automatic to a neighbour, who was delighted with it. With a modern single-bed machine, as well as a double-bed, my knitting scope was widened enormously.

I wanted to write about machine knitting — to let other women know of its immense possibilities — so I wrote the story of Mary Weaver (who runs the Weaverknit Centre in Kent) for the magazine *Woman*, and this brought in a flood of letters from knitters and would-be knitters, and made me more sure than ever that machine knitting is today's hobby.

As a result of this story, Knitmaster asked me to write a 'chat' column in their magazine *Modern Knitting*, so from July 1972 until January 1977 I wrote 'Woolgathering' (under my pen name 'Sally') for them. This brought me so many warm and friendly letters from all over the country (and abroad) that when, in February 1977, my 'Woolgathering' ceased to be a part of *Modern Knitting*, I decided to continue it privately, and I am hoping in this way to keep in touch with my many knitting friends.

During the years I worked with *Modern Knitting*, I naturally learned to use Knitmaster machines. I now have a 326, a 323 and a 250, and I like them very much.

It may seem extravagant to have so many machines (and of course one good machine is quite sufficient — though two are fun!) but machine knitting is now very tied up with my working life as a writer, and I also run a tiny cottage industry, to raise money for charity, so it is an advantage for me to understand a number of machines. All the machines I own and use are good. They all produce beautiful work; they all have some special quality.

The longer I knit — and write about knitting — the more knitters I meet, the more letters I receive. And again and again I hear: "We want more reading matter about our hobby. Not just patterns, but hints, and ideas, and how to overcome snags, and other knitters' experiences . . . why don't you write a book about the wonderful things a knitting machine can do?"

This seemed a lovely idea. I couldn't wait to begin . . .

And yet I knew that not all machine-owners are machine-knitters. Far too many machines are pushed under the spare room bed; far too many owners feel they've wasted their money. It seems to me that a book about machine knitting should help them, too, and show them what they've been missing.

Here is the book. I have two wishes for it: that keen knitters should enjoy it, and that frustrated knitters should let it persuade them to get out their abandoned machines and have another go. I should be really happy if only a few of them wrote and told me: "Have machine. Can knit".

Jane Anthony
Old Quarry
Keysworth
Wareham
Dorset

1
Machine Knitting is Today's Hobby

Machine knitting is booming, for three main reasons:

A Knitting Machine Saves Money

It keeps spending down, and standards up: a machine knitter can make more — and better — clothes for herself and her family for less money than she would spend in the shops.

Concrete examples are better than generalisations, so: This year (1977) I have made beautiful Shetland wool sweaters for myself (34" - 85 cm) for as little as £1.10 and for my husband (42" - 105 cm) for £1.52. Synthetic garments are even cheaper: I recently made six children's cardigans from one cone of pink Courtelle, bought in the market for 60p.

Knitwear is not only a 'must' in our climate — it is top fashion. Look in the glossy magazines and expensive boutiques. A lot of this knitwear is actually made on a home knitting machine — the sort that you and I can quickly learn to use. The knitting machine makes everything — tough sweaters to do the gardening in, lurex evening outfits, casually elegant suits, play sweaters, sports wear, bikinis, house coats. It makes for the home as well as for the family. The modern machines weave, and you can cut this material out and make it up on your sewing machine. Usually, the cost of making your curtains and covers on the knitting machine works out well under half the cost of bought material. I recently made two beautiful cushion covers for under £2.50 — in the shops they would have cost over £5 (and mine were nicer!) A reader wrote proudly to tell me she had made a beautiful white cotton bedspread, double size, for under £2, and that she had seen similar ones — *single size* — for £8.80.

The knitting machine is the perfect answer to present giving. In 1975

When children have special interests — like riding, skating, ballet lessons — the clothes they need are not cheap. But these two young horsewomen are wearing original sweaters that cost 80p for the larger size, 55p for the smaller. They were knitted by their mother, on a Knitmaster 323. She used 4-ply acrylic yarn, and a friend at her knitting club (Metropolitan Sewing Machine Co of Bournemouth) designed the punch card.

Christmas presents I gave included: a real Shetland shawl for an old lady — cost 96p. Shetland shawls in the shops were from £5 to £11. A woven knitting bag — cost £1.18 including the wooden handles — less attractive bags were selling at £3.50. A fisherman's rib coat for a friend's small elderly dog — cost 48p; poorer quality ones were selling in the shops for £1.50. Several fair isle tank tops — cost around £1.00 each. These were in good quality wool — similar garments in cheap synthetics were selling for around £3.50.

A knitting machine adds a touch of luxury . . . last winter I admired (in a London store) a simple tank top in brown lambswool, with a faint scribble of gold — it was just what I wanted to wear with a silk shirt for evenings. BUT it was £19. I copied it on my machine for £1.50. And mine fitted me perfectly: the one I saw in the shop would have been a little too long.

A Knitting Machine Makes Money

and it makes it in a very flexible way. There is scope for the woman who simply wants to make a few extra pounds, without leaving her home, and for the woman who thinks big and wants to build up her own business.

There are some good stories behind the big names in machine knitting. But this book is concerned mainly with the spare-time earner. People like Mrs. B., whose health is poor; she cannot go out to work but has managed, with her knitting machine, to earn herself some of the extras her husband's wage does not cover: a sewing machine, a new cooker, a refrigerator. Mrs. G., whose spare time is very limited, makes just enough in those few hours to pay the rental on a colour television for her invalid husband. Mrs. F. pays for the family holidays. Mrs. C. has had to be breadwinner since her husband's accident, and manages to earn £25 to £30 a week — while still caring for her husband and home. There are men, too, who earn with their machines: one pensioner of over eighty regularly makes £5 to £6 a week; this makes all the difference, he says, between "just managing" and living comfortably.

I also know of people who want to make money with their knitting machines, and have so far not been able to. Later in this book I want to talk about some reasons for failure, and how these can be overcome.

A Knitting Machine is a Way of Life

Machine knitting saves and makes money. It can also be a refuge.

"Gradually I came alive again," wrote one knitter. She had suffered a terrible loss, felt nothing was worth while, was persuaded to take up machine knitting and agreed "because it was better than just sitting and staring." And *slowly* she became interested, even keen. That was the beginning of recovery.

I have a thick file of letters very like that one. They come from people who have met serious misfortune — bereavement, divorce, desertion, ill health — and found that a creative hobby opens an escape hatch out of misery. Most of these women simply did not have the money to take up hobbies such as pottery or painting or sculpture — they'd have felt selfish if they'd bought the equipment, or taken time off to learn and practise. But knitting is immediately useful and practical. It can save and make money, and so help the family budget.

Once again it is the flexibility of machine knitting that puts it in a special class. Some people are helped by the soothing repetitive action of turning out standard garments. Others need a challenge — decide to go into business for themselves. Others need human contacts, and are attracted to tutoring or demonstrating. Some find they have a strong creative streak, and take up designing.

I sincerely hope that you — reading this — will not be faced with the sort of unhappiness that makes some form of escape essential. But if ever you are, your knitting machine can help you.

But it would be silly to pretend that there are no problems or disappointments in machine knitting. Silly — and unrealistic. Because most of us have heard of at least one disillusioned owner, who has a machine that is pushed out of sight because she "can't get on with the thing."

These facts should not be hidden under the carpet, but brought out, examined and explained. This is the purpose of the next chapter.

2
What can go Wrong?

I believe there are three main reasons for people failing to make good use of their knitting machines.

Tuition
Technical Hitches
Home Circumstances.

Tuition

(You should check carefully, when you buy a knitting machine, what tuition is available — see Chapter Four: *Choosing a knitting machine*. In this chapter I am talking to the woman who already has a machine, but for one reason or another did not get the tuition she needed.)

If your machine is a current model, still being produced, then tuition is available. Contact the shop where you bought your machine, and if they cannot help, contact the maker. State clearly why you have not had tuition — if it was your own fault, don't be afraid to say so — and ask what can be done, now, to put matters right. If there has been some slip on the part of the shop, or the maker, a polite factual letter should get cooperation. If the fault was yours, then no doubt tuition can be arranged, and even if you have to pay for it, it is surely better than leaving your machine lying idle, when it could be saving and earning money.

If the tuition is by postal course, or instruction book only, and you have lost this, tell the makers what has happened and ask them to help you. You may have to pay for a new book, or course, but it is money well spent.

If your machine is now obsolete, it may still be a good machine, but it may be more difficult to get tuition. If the firm that made it is still in business, write to them — they may have someone on their staff who can solve problems for you, they may even have a tutor who remembers the model and could give you a couple of lessons. If the firm is no longer in business, you must look elsewhere for help.

Some local authorities now run evening classes on machine knitting — enquire at your evening institute. Even if no such class exists, they may be willing to start one if there is a demand. Enquire and advertise to see if you can find other would-be knitters in your area.

Most areas have at least one knitting club. Try to locate this: you could enquire from machine knitting dealers, or wool shops, or put a card in a shop window or a small advertisement in a local paper. Or the women's page editor on your local paper might know of any such group. If you can find a club, you may very well be able to get the help you need. Knitters are usually friendly people, delighted to share their hobby, and even if none of them is familiar with your machine, some of the more experienced knitters will probably be able to see how it works.

Unless you live in a very isolated spot, or are unable to leave your home, you stand a good chance of getting at least some help. But if that fails, then get out the instruction book, make up your mind you are going to master the machine, take just one process at a time, and practise this until you are really proficient before going on to the next step.

Unfortunately some owners of older machines never get past the first step — casting on — because they find this difficult to do and complain that stitches are dropped or missed, and that it is impossible to achieve a neat edge.

This brings us to number two on our list:

Technical Hitches

Sometimes the reason is very simple: beginners want to knit with a fairly small stitch size (to make a nice firm fabric) and their (old) instruction books do not always warn them that the casting-on row should always be fairly loose — not less than, say, 7 for a 4-ply — more for thicker yarns. But it may be more serious than that.

Casting-on troubles were fairly common with some of the early machines. And even though the faults usually right themselves, after the first few rows, there is something very depressing about starting off a piece of knitting with an ugly, uneven edge, which will have to be 'cobbled up' or concealed later.

You remember the little boy who was told that his new shoes might hurt for the first day, so he didn't wear them until the second day . . .

If the knitting is poor on the first few rows, but improves after that, then

Larger sizes take a long, long time to knit by hand; the knitting machine is so fast that even outsizes can be made in hours rather than weeks. Not only that, but larger sizes (for men and women) are difficult to find and very expensive in the shops. Some knitters have built up a wide circle of customers by specialising in large sizes: their order books are full, and their customers — tired of being told "not in your size" — are very grateful.

do away with the first few rows. This can be done with the 'waste yarn' method. This is regularly used on modern machines, but some of the people who wrote the instructions for early machines seem not to have heard of it.

Casting on with waste (or contrast) yarn means that the actual casting-on, and the knitting of the first few rows (where some machines drop or miss stitches) is done with an oddment of wool, roughly the same thickness as the yarn in which you will be knitting the garment, but of a different colour. In this way, if there are dropped or missed stitches, causing an untidy edge, they will occur in the waste yarn, which is discarded later. You do not start knitting with the main yarn until these snags have ironed themselves out — which means that your first row knitted in main yarn should be perfect.

Follow the maker's instructions for casting on — but use waste or contrast yarn. Now start knitting, again following instructions. You may find your old machine has dropped or missed stitches. But you can pick up dropped loops and place them on the needles, and where a needle has missed a stitch you can lift a loop from the row below, on to the needle, and it should knit perfectly on the next row (sometimes it 'picks up' all by itself). Your edge may still be uneven and untidy — just what always discouraged you before — but now that untidy edge is in waste yarn, which *will not form part of the finished garment.*

Keep knitting, still with waste yarn. When you have a perfect row — no dropped or missed stitches — then knit a few more rows, to be on the safe side, and then, with the cam box on the left, knit one row with the casting-on cord (I will explain this later. See page 14.) Then, with your cam box on the right, change to main yarn, and start knitting in accordance with the pattern you are following.

When you have finished your hem, or mock rib welt, your instructions will probably tell you to lift the cast-on stitches on to the needles, thus closing the hem. But if you have started with waste yarn, then you will lift the loops of the first row knitted in main yarn — that is, the first row after the row knitted with the casting-on cord — on to the corresponding needles.

The sketch shows you how to do this.

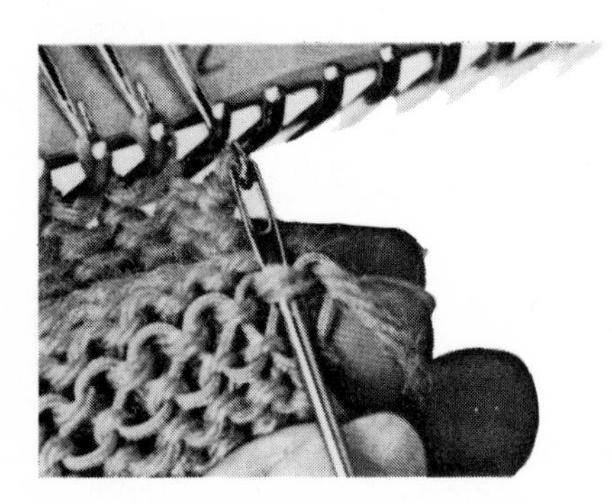

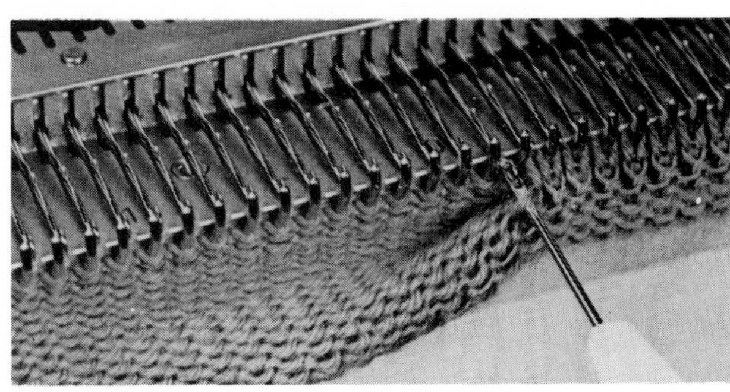

This is often referred to as 'make a hem' or 'make a double edge'. Remember that if you are making a plain stocking stitch hem, knitting on every needle, then after you have lifted the loops (or stitches) there will be two stitches on every needle, so knit the first row very slowly and make sure every needle knits properly. With thick or difficult yarns I sometimes knit this row by hand, but this is not often necessary.

Next, I usually knit one more row and then pull out the casting-on cord, taking care not to strain the needles. Some knitters prefer to knit several rows before removing the cord.

If you have made a mock rib welt — say two needles in working position, one needle in non-working position all along the row — then before you lift the loops you should push the empty needles up into working position. Make sure you put a loop on to each one of these empty needles.

Your mock rib welt may seem loose and shapeless, but this (assuming you have used the right stitch size) is only because the stitches need to be pulled together. Modern machines sometimes supply a special rib bar — but you can use a narrow ruler, or a thick knitting needle, or a thin smooth piece of dowelling (although something with a flat edge — such as the ruler — is really better). Slide this into the fold of the welt, hold the main part of the knitting firmly in one hand, the ruler in the other, and give a firm strong downward pull. Do not tug and jerk, just pull firmly. If you are using wool, you can do this in the steam of a boiling kettle (watch your hands) or over a sink full of hot water, but this treatment could harm some synthetics.

You will see how the stitches close up, giving a much more 'ribbed' appearance. The welt itself will be longer (sometimes more than twice the length it was when it came off the knitting machine) and considerably narrower. Modern instruction books explain this clearly, but some instruction books for older machines did not make it clear, so that knitters had another cause for discouragement: they felt it was impossible to achieve a good-looking ribbed-effect welt, and concluded that they would either have to buy a ribbing attachment or knit welts by hand.

In fact these mock rib welts, properly done and stretched, look really good. Many knitters prefer them to 'real' ribbing on double bed machine or ribbing attachment, because as there is no closed-edge cast-on, garments started in this way stand up better to children (of all ages!) who tug their sweaters over their heads, push the cuffs halfway up their arms and generally put a strain on the cast-on edge which may mean broken stitches.

Even today, some machine knitting patterns designed for simple machines start by saying: "Using size . . . knitting needles, work . . . rows in k.1.p.1 rib . . ." and this makes me really angry. It implies that you cannot do a satisfactory welt on a simple knitting machine — which is simply not true.

If for any reason you want a closed-edge cast on, you can still use the waste yarn method. Cast on with waste yarn, knit until you have several perfect rows, knit one row with the casting-on cord — all as already described — and then, following the instructions in your instruction book, cast on again but this time with main yarn. This is not as foolproof a way as the first method, but it is quite often successful. If you have difficulty with this, and still want a firm cast-on, try this way:

Cast on with waste yarn, knit until you have some perfect rows, knit one row with the casting-on cord, continue knitting in main. When you have finished your piece of knitting and removed it from the machine, turn it upside down, place the stitches of the first row knitted in main yarn on to the needles, remove waste yarn, and cast off following the instructions in your book. If you wish to make a hem, you will then have to slip-stitch this into position (or use one of the methods suggested under *Hems* in Chapter Fourteen).

Or you can pick up the first row knitted in main yarn on to knitting needles of a suitable size, and cast off by hand. This sounds like a contradiction, after what I have said about the use of knitting needles, but in fact casting off, on a knitting machine, is about the only operation that I find nearly as slow as hand-knitting. When you are a little more proficient, you will usually be able to avoid this chore altogether. But while you are still a beginner, you may sometimes find a hand cast-off helpful. Remember — this is only a temporary prop, until you have learned other ways of coping. And remember too that this particular problem — untidy cast-on — does not arise with the good *modern* machine.

In all these methods, *the waste yarn has to be removed* — and this is the reason for the casting-on cord. You could remove the waste yarn simply by unravelling it, but the casting-on cord is quicker.

Manufacturers now usually supply this cord. It is a fine, strong, smooth cord, about the thickness of a 2-ply knitting yarn. But you can use anything similar: some silky crochet cottons are good, or knitting rayon (as long as it does not break easily), even a very strong sewing thread. I have also successfully used ordinary 3-ply knitting nylon. Anything will do, as long as it is soft and pliable (so as not to damage the needles) and smooth enough to be pulled out of the knitting without snagging or puckering.

When you have completed your hem, take hold of one end of the casting-on cord and pull gently and firmly. The cord should slide through the work, and the waste yarn will be separated from the main yarn.

Never strain the needles as you pull the cord. This could damage them. If for any reason the cord does not slide out smoothly, trace back carefully to where the trouble is. It may be that the cord has wrapped itself round a needle, or a stitch. It is usually simple to disentangle this, using the appropriate tool or a wool needle with a blunt tip.

If you do not wish to make a hem — for example if you wish to graft two lots of stitches together or if you wish to turn the hem to the outside and back stitch into the open loops (see Chapter Eight) then complete the piece of knitting, remove it from the machine, and press the first few rows after the casting-on cord. With wool you can use a hot iron and damp cloth, with some synthetics you must use a cool iron and dry cloth, with other synthetics pressing may be harmful. In this case, either dampen the area, and allow it to dry naturally, or run strong sewing cotton through the first row of stitches knitted in the main yarn. The object is the same in all cases — to prevent the stitches from running when the casting-on cord is pulled out.

Another frequent complaint from new knitters is that *'the stitches jump off the needles'* (I have heard this complaint about good modern machines, as well as 'oldies') and although this does not really happen, it is true that stitches and needles may occasionally part company — which naturally throws the inexperienced knitter into a panic.

There are several reasons for 'jumping stitches':

(*a*) the knitted fabric may be too light in weight. This means that the knitting rides up (there is nothing to hold it down) and the stitches slip off the needles.

Modern knitting machines (and some old ones) have strippers, brushes or weights to hold the knitting down. But right at the beginning of a piece of knitting there may simply not be enough fabric for these aids to work on. Casting on with waste yarn sometimes helps — this means that before you begin to knit with main yarn, there will be an inch or so of knitting, which may be sufficiently 'weighty' to hold the stitches down. These waste rows also provide something to hang the weights on (if your machine uses weights) or casting-on comb.

Even if no weights are supplied with your machine, you may find that weighting your knitting is helpful. I am afraid some manufacturers may be annoyed with me for saying this, but after knitting for fifteen years I can see nothing against it, as long as you use the minimum amount of weight, just sufficient to keep the knitting hanging straight down and overcome any tendency to ride up. Too much weight is bad — fine fabrics can be distorted; sometimes the damage cannot be put right. Too much weight, it is claimed, also causes dropped stitches to run and form ladders. But I have never found the right amount of weight do this (and in any case, as you become more proficient, dropped stitches will be very rare indeed, and quickly dealt with *if* they should occur).

If your knitting rides up, and the stitches come off the needles (and assuming that you are using a machine that does not provide weights) then try an experiment: knit with one hand and use the other to hold the knitting down — gently but quite firmly. If this solves the problem, then buy and use some weights.

Weights do not fit on to the machine itself — they merely hook into the knitting — so that you can use the weights made for a different make of machine. A good knitting machine dealer should be able to supply some. All you need are the usual type which come with single bed machines (weight around 4 oz - 113.4 gm) — there are larger and heavier ones, but these are usually for ribbing attachments or for extra thick yarns.

(*b*) Stitches sometimes come off the needles because the yarn brake is not set correctly. If it pulls the wool up too tightly, it will be impossible for the machine to knit complete stitches of the correct size. As your cam box moves across the bed, the stitches may become smaller and tighter (because the machine is being starved of yarn) until finally the machine is not able to knit at all — and the work comes off the needles.

It may help beginners to work a few rows very, very slowly, and watch what happens: the yarn is placed in the hook of the needle, the needle comes forward to receive it and then slides back so as to pull the yarn through the loop of the stitch on the previous row. Unless the yarn flows freely — so that the machine can carry out all these operations — there can be no good knitting.

Your instruction book will tell you how to set the yarn brake and tension spring for various thicknesses of yarn, but (as with stitch sizes) these settings are for guidance and not necessarily to be followed exactly. If you find you have some problem with the flow of the yarn, try this simple test: pull the yarn (behind the mast) gently down until the tension spring is pointing sharply downwards towards the bed of the machine. Let go of the yarn. The spring should rise slowly until it is approximately horizontal. If it stays right down, the yarn tension is too tight. If it flips straight up in the air, it is too loose. When the tension is too tight, the edge stitches will not knit properly and the work may come off the machine. When the tension is too loose, you will get ugly loops at the edge of your work (because the tension spring is not lifting the yarn up and out of the way).

(*c*) Another reason for stitches 'jumping off the needles' is that inexperienced knitters do not always take the cam box far enough across the bed. Study your instruction book again — make sure you understand how far the cam box should be taken. Some instructions tell you to listen for the small 'click' that means you have gone far enough, others advise a certain distance. Again, it helps to knit a few rows very slowly, and watch what happens. You will see that once the last needle has been completely cleared, the yarn is ready for the return trip — in the opposite direction. If you take your cam box too far beyond the last needle, your wool is likely to loop (giving an untidy edge). But if you do not take it far enough, the yarn is not in the right position to knit the first stitch of the next row. What often happens, with beginners, is that they start slowly and carefully, and all is well. Then they gain confidence, find out how easy and quick it is, speed up, and — disaster! The stitches are off the needles. This is because they have started to knit back before the wool is correctly positioned for the next row. In effect, they are following the instructions for 'stripping off' (removing the work from the machine). Remember that knitting across, without yarn, removes the knitting from the needles.

If you have trouble with stitches coming off the needles, check all these points:

(*a*) is your fabric too light — is it riding up and so slipping off the needles?

(*b*) is the yarn tension too tight, so that the yarn is being snatched up and this in turn is pulling the stitches off the needles?

(*c*) are you taking the cam box far enough across the bed, on every row?

Usually, attention to these points solves the problem.

But stitches may sometimes come off the needle because they are too tight (small) or too loose (large). Sometimes new knitters are so absorbed in the actual process of knitting — for the first few times — that they don't really see what they are producing. A piece of machine knitting is like a piece of hand knitting in that it should be pleasantly firm and close, but NOT stiff and tight. If you feel that your knitting is too tight or too loose, take an oddment of yarn and experiment with different stitch sizes, until you produce a fabric that pleases you. Of course, if you alter the stitch size, you will alter the finished size of whatever you are knitting — but I shall explain all this in Chapter Eleven.

Another possible reason for disappointment and failure is that you may be using unsuitable yarn. This applies to new, as well as old machines.

You cannot do good knitting with harsh, hairy, coarse, stiff yarn. Even experienced knitters could not achieve good results with this (they are too experienced to try, anyway) but some beginners expect to.

If you feel this may be your difficulty, turn to Chapter Thirteen and read more about the yarns that are suitable for knitting machines.

Some beginners, who realise that harsh coarse yarns will not produce good work, think that if they use good quality yarn they will get good results — even if that good yarn has been made up, washed (probably more than once), unravelled, steamed, re-wound, re-knitted . . . in short when it has already seen a good deal of wear and tear. Skilled knitters can, and do, re-use old wool, and make lovely things with it. But the combination of very old yarn with very new knitter is not a good one. Until you are a little more experienced, treat yourself to some nice *new* yarn — you will save the cost many, many times once you have learned to use your machine.

Another yarn trap is that beginners — hearing how cheap the coned synthetic yarns are, how well they knit up, what beautiful colours they are made in — rush out and buy themselves a huge cone of very fine synthetic yarn (and get into difficulties). This is one of the pleasantest yarns to work with — smooth and easy — but usually it has to be used several thicknesses at a time. Child's play — when you've done a little machine knitting. But not for your first few garments. Again, treat yourself to some nice smooth 3- or 4-ply yarn. It is money well spent.

Unless you use coned wool — wound for machine knitting — rewind your wool with the wool-winder which is an essential companion to your knitting machine. You cannot machine-knit from balls of wool wound for handknitting. The yarn you use to begin with ought to be so smooth and trouble free that waxing will not be necessary. But remember — as you use a wider variety of yarns — that some quite good yarns benefit by waxing. This is just holding a piece of wax in your left hand, and allowing the wool to run over the wax as you wind. Waxing does not mean that you can use harsh, whiskery, unsuitable yarns on your machine — they can harm it and they are not worth knitting up in any case. But it does mean that some good yarns, which tend otherwise to be just a little rough, can be knitted smoothly and easily.

I am not claiming that every old machine tucked away in some one's attic is capable of doing good work. Some models, of course, were better than others. Some — now out of production — may have had serious faults. But I do believe that most old machines can do good work within their limits.

Quite often it is one of these points — difficulty in casting on, stitches coming off the needles, using unsuitable yarn — that puts the new knitter (with an old machine) off knitting. And quite often these faults can be cured.

Home circumstances

are often to blame when a woman who was really keen to have, and to use, a knitting machine loses heart and gives up.

Knitting machines are still fairly new. And the word 'machine' still conjures up the idea of something that needs a fair amount of mechanical skill. And there is still — in far, far too many families — a tendency to think of dear old Mum as a bit of a dunderhead. Of course she is a super cook, and can make beds and wash up — but "honestly, can you see her coping with one of those complicated things . . . ?" I know of several cases where insensitive and not-over-bright husbands and families have made it impossible for a new machine owner to learn to use her machine. They crowded round the tutor, asking flippant questions; they 'hovered' obviously wanting the table, or longing to turn on the television. Or they just watched — silently and pityingly, while the poor learner struggled with new techniques, until she was all fingers and thumbs and wished she had never heard of knitting machines.

Sometimes the tuition goes smoothly: the new owner actually learns how to use her machine, and feels reasonably confident that she can make things on it. But though Dad has his shed or his garage, and more and more children and teenagers are having their bedrooms turned into play rooms or studies, there is often no provision at all for the mother of the family to have a hobby. She puts her sewing or knitting machine on the kitchen or dining room table — and just as she is getting on famously, it is time to prepare or serve a meal. Even with a sewing machine this is a nuisance. We all know what a difference it makes to have a tiny sewing corner where work can be left, and returned to. With a knitting machine it is even more important. If the machine has to be moved, the cam box may have to be taken off, the mast and tension spring dismantled. If there is a piece of knitting on the machine, this may be damaged — stitches may be dropped, loose ends of wool may catch and drag; knobs and levers may be knocked, the row counter flipped forwards or backwards; in short, the odds are heavily against the knitter who does not have a corner — however small — of her own where her machine can be set up permanently.

I shall be talking about this — and making some suggestions — in Chapter Five.

If you are going to make a success of machine knitting you must take a realistic attitude towards it. Simply getting your old machine out from its hiding place, or even buying yourself a brand new one, is not enough. No machine can knit all by itself. It is YOU, plus your machine, that will produce beautiful things.

So be clear from the beginning: you must have space (however small) and you must have time (however little).

You may have to be firm with your family. You may have to reorganise your own working schedule. And right at the beginning, when you are producing nothing more than small pieces of fabric — and sometimes even those go wrong — it is easy to let yourself be talked out of the idea, or even to talk yourself out of it. But later, when you are producing lovely clothes and household furnishings, for less than half what you'd pay in the shops (and possibly making some money as well) you will know it was worth while — AND the family jibes will die down.

Nothing is for nothing. Machine knitting can bring you a great deal of pleasure and profit. But YOU have to make the effort, in the beginning.

I can imagine some of you, at this stage, feeling that you'd really like to have another go at machine knitting. And then hesitating . . .

Is it really worth while, you'll ask yourselves, to master one of the old machines, when the modern machines can do so much more? Will you be restricted, with your earlier model, to very plain, down-to-earth knitting — and so lose interest?

Of course, if you can easily spare the money, go and buy the machine of your choice, regardless of price. The modern machines *are* wonderful — there is no doubt about that. But if for any reason you cannot — or don't want to — buy a new machine, then I believe it is certainly well worth while to make the most of the old one. Even if your machine is limited to plain stocking stitch — as long as it is clean, oiled and in good working order — you can make beautiful knitwear on it.

I know of many people turning out excellent work on a basic machine; some of them sell their knitwear; some of them have earned enough, in this way, to buy a modern machine.

In the next chapter I want to tell you some of the things you can do with one of the basic machines.

3
Making the most of a Simple Machine

This book is for all machine knitters — and that includes many people who own one of the older, basic machines.

These machines will not do the wonderful things that some of the modern machines can do. But they can still produce very attractive knitwear.

Plain does not mean dull. Look in some of the best knitwear shops, and you will see that some of the most attractive and expensive knitwear is in plain stocking stitch, with hem, neckbands etc in the same stitch or in reversed stocking stitch, or in a simple rib (and even basic machines can do mock ribbing).

If you have an old machine, you cannot do all-over fair isle or other stitch patterns, or big bold motifs with the ease of a modern punch card machine. But you can do a lot to add interest to your knitting:

Random or flecked yarns, tweed mixtures and some of the bouclés knit up as well on an old machine (and look as good) as on a new one. To begin with you may want to buy a luxury yarn, like Jaeger 'Matchmaker', but later you will no doubt try making your own mix-and-match effects, by using several strands of fine coned yarns. (It's worth remembering that — with a machine that does only plain knitting — the actual texture of the yarn will be very noticeable, and sometimes it pays to be extravagant.)

Several strands of different coloured fine yarn knitted in plain stocking stitch and made up on the reverse side, can look like fine tweed, if you are clever with your colours.

Cables are very effective — they will have to be worked by hand, but this is true of new machines, too.

Embroidery and Swiss darning add colour and interest. A knitter I know, with a very simple machine, recently made a pale blue Shetland wool sweater with a big roll collar. The design was for an automatic machine, and featured a row of stylised flowers running from the welt, right over the shoulder to the back welt. But the owner of a basic machine copied it and instead of the panel of fair isle she Swiss darned white snowflakes where the pattern indicated fair isle. This was so successful that she made another similar sweater — cherry red — and this time she used simple embroidery stitches and worked a yoke of lazy daisies in white, and pale blue, with yellow centres.

Other attractive ideas I have seen — carried out on a simple machine — include: a V-necked jacket in Aran white double knitting. No hem, cuffs, welts or knitted front bands, but the whole garment bordered with five rows of double crochet (two scarlet, one Aran white, two navy). It is easy to make buttonholes in this type of crochet edging: decide where you want them to be, miss 3 (or more) d.c. then do 3 ch. and continue in d.c. On the next row, you work d.c. into the chain; a fine-knit black sweater, embroidered with a simple design in tiny gold beads; a low-necked sweater with the neckline outlined in small crocheted flowers; plain sweaters Swiss-darned to give the effect of vertical stripes — used with horizontal knitted-in stripes this makes checks; poncho-pulls with matching or contrasting fringes and/or with big bold motifs added; fringes — in the same colour as the garment, in a contrast, or multi-coloured — used to trim the edge of a big loose collar; trouser suits in plain dark colours with bands of stripes round trouser bottoms and waistline of sweater.

With plain garments, whether or not you add interest in various ways, it is very important to aim at a perfect finish. This is important with all knitwear, but details which may be unnoticeable in a brilliant all-over fair isle garment stand out sharply in a plain one. So be sure to do fully fashioned shaping wherever this improves the appearance of a garment — and when possible make the decreases four or five stitches in, rather than the two or three which simple patterns often give. This means that the fifth stitch from each edge will be moved on to the sixth needle from each edge (the sixth needle will have two stitches on it) the remaining stitches will be moved up, and the empty (edge) needle put back into non-working position.

You can often still further improve the appearance of a garment *and* save time by decreasing two stitches at a time, which means you need decrease only half as many times. See Chapter Seven.

Knitters who try out this more interesting way of shaping sometimes say that the edges of the raglans are drawn up too tightly, so that the seam puckers. If this happens to you, check carefully to see that yarn brake and tension spring are set correctly, for the yarn you are using. And sometimes hanging a small weight on the edge stitches, moving it up every few rows, cures the trouble.

But do not make elaborate, fully fashioned shapings where they will not show — this is a waste of time. In some fancy yarns, such as bouclé, fully fashioned shaping is unnoticeable. When you make your tension square for a garment knitted in a yarn like this, do a few more inches and try the effect of fully fashioned shaping. If it improves the appearance, use it. If not, decrease in the quick and easy way by putting the edge stitch on to the next needle and putting the edge needle out of working position.

So far we have been assuming that you will be knitting — with your simple machine — mainly classic garments. But don't forget that plain stocking stitch — in the right yarn and colour — can do everything that a fine expensive jersey material can do. Start with a basic, classic pattern by all means; use it to gain confidence (as well as to make some nice garments). But quite soon you can branch out, if you wish. You can alter the neck line, make the whole garment longer or shorter, shape it in at the waist. Try deep square armholes, with wide sleeves that hang loosely or are gathered into a cuff; knit a long straight kaftan and cinch it in at the waist with a chain belt; add length (and width, unless you are very slim) to a sleeveless pullover pattern and make a pinafore dress.

4
Choosing a Machine

I have already told you that I have five machines, and that I like them all. But I certainly don't want to tell you which machine to buy — only to give you some pointers to help you make the right choice for yourself.

It is a big purchase. Take your time. Write to the manufacturers for their literature, the name of their nearest stockist, and particulars of tuition available. Study the leaflets carefully, then go and look at the machines. The good stockist is an enthusiast, so don't be afraid to ask questions, ask for a demonstration and — if you are seriously interested — try out the machines for yourself.

You should check on these points:

Is patterning *really* easy?

Is it easy (and quick) to put needles into holding position (you will need to do this very often, for shaping necks, shoulders, darts etc)?

Is the machine smooth and pleasant to work with? You'll be pushing that carriage to and fro thousands of times — it *must* work properly.

Does it produce beautiful, even fabric, with neat edges?

Check on the tuition available. Can you spread it out into short lessons? Can you go back and ask for help if you run into difficulties?

What extras will you need? For instance, you will need a wool winder — is this included in the price? You must have a rigid table — unless there is something suitable in your home, or a handyman can make something for you, you may have to buy a knitting machine table. Make sure that, when you get your machine home, with such extras as you have decided to buy, you will be all set to knit.

You should also check on what patterns are available for your machine. However, patterns come and go — new ones are always being worked out, and I think it would be a mistake to be put off the machine you really like just because the patterns are not entirely to your taste. *The main thing is to get the machine you will be happy with.* There are plenty of easy patterns suitable for most makes of machines (see Chapter Twelve) and, much sooner than you think, you will be adapting patterns written for other makes, or even hand-knitting patterns, or designing your own simple — and then more sophisticated — patterns.

All the manufacturers I have mentioned have their own magazine or pattern books, which appear at different intervals. You may look through just one issue of one of these publications and decide the designs are too young, too old, too trendy, too classic etc for your taste. But no publication can please every single person in every single issue. In my opinion it is well worth subscribing to the publication that covers your machine. *This* issue may have nothing that appeals to you; *the next* issue may be crammed with just the kind of patterns you like. Even when the pattern itself is not one you want to knit, read through it: you may find making-up hints, stitch patterns, and all sorts of interesting know-how. In my view, these publications are value for money.

So far we have been assuming you want to buy a new machine. But many knitters start off with a secondhand machine. As with everything else secondhand, you take a risk, and need to be careful.

If there is a good knitting machine centre near you, see if they have any used machines that they can recommend. They often take machines in part exchange, and these are sometimes fairly new models. For instance, when Knitmaster brought out the 323, many people sold their 321 models, to buy the newer one, and there were some good bargains to be had. When you buy from a reputable stockist you will be able to go back — if something should go wrong — and ask to have it put right. Ask about this before buying.

If you buy privately, you *could* waste your money — or you could buy a machine that will give you years of perfect knitting. Don't be tempted by cheapness alone. The shorter you are of money, the more careful you should be.

Look carefully at the needles — are they bent or twisted? Are any of the latches missing? It is true that damaged needles can be replaced quite easily, on most models. But if several needles are damaged it could be that the machine has had rather rough treatment, and other damage may have been done.

Try to find out why the vendor is parting with her machine. Perhaps she has used it a good deal, but is now progressing to a more modern machine. If the old one has been treated with respect and kept clean and oiled, it may give years of good service, and be a real bargain. Perhaps some misfortune — failing eyesight, arthritis etc — makes knitting difficult, and again you may get a really good buy. Perhaps the vendor bought — or was given — the machine on an impulse, and has never really got interested . . . there are all sorts of legitimate reasons for selling a knitting machine. *But* — it may not have been a very good machine in the first place. Or the owner may have handled it carelessly and bent and twisted needles or damaged the cam box. Or the children may have lost some of the vital tools, or gummed up the works by spilling cocoa into it. Find out as much as you can about the reason for selling, and use your judgment as to whether you are being given the real reason. All this sounds nasty and suspicious, and you may feel embarrassed. But the would-be vendor has offered her machine for sale; it is perfectly reasonable for the prospective buyer to want to know exactly what she will get for her money.

Ask for a demonstration, and then try it out for yourself, exactly as if you were buying a new machine.

Check on tuition — is the instruction book complete, and is it clear? Is the machine still in production (which usually means you can get tuition)? Can the vendor teach you — and is she willing to do so? Make quite sure on this point — a lot of people sell good machines because they have never taken the trouble to learn how to use them.

Do not buy unless the machine produces nice even fabric, and make sure that all the 'bits and pieces' are there (the instruction book should have a list, often with drawings of the various tools etc). Also find out whether the makers are still in business, (even if the machine is no longer being made) and whether spares are available.

Do not buy if the machine is stiff, jerky and altogether a misery to use. I know people who have bought secondhand machines that were — and have remained — difficult to operate. The vendors persuaded them that "it is only stiff, because it hasn't been used for so long . . ." This could be quite true, but it is up to the owner to clean and oil and work the machine and make sure it is NOT stiff before she asks anyone to pay good money for it. If this excuse is handed out, say politely that you'll come again — *after* the machine has been cleaned and oiled and got into good working order. You may then find that it works like a dream. If it is still stiff and jerky — forget it. Any machine that grinds and sticks and takes all the pleasure out of knitting (after it has been cleaned and oiled) is not a good buy.

If you buy from someone who has never learned to use her machine, then you will be on your own as regards tuition. See Chapter Two for suggestions on how to get help in the early stages.

5
A Place to Knit

Nothing holds a knitter back from success more than having to pack up and put away her machine between each knitting session. Not only can work be damaged, and machine settings accidentally altered, but it is a depressing chore and may make you dread your knitting, rather than eagerly looking forward to it.

Another important point is that most of us do not have our spare time in one long period, but in odd hours and half-hours. If you have to set up and dismantle your machine for every knitting session, the short periods simply cannot be used to good advantage. Most of your time will be spent getting out and putting away the machine!

Of course, the ideal is a spare room, but there are alternatives: under the stairs, in a large alcove, using a room divider in a living or bedroom that is larger than necessary, curtaining or partitioning off waste space in a hall or on a landing. A handyman can sometimes make a good looking fitment that opens out into a knitting unit. Some knitters go outside the house — one ingenious lady turned her disused coal hole into a super little workroom and I know of two who use, all winter, the family's holiday caravan.

But whether you have the luxury of a whole room, or have to squeeze into a corner, you must have:

Good light. Daylight is ideal, but most of us have to knit in the evenings. I like a fluorescent tube light, fixed above my machine. I can see well, and it consumes less electricity than a powerful bulb.

A rigid table. You cannot do good work with the table wobbling and the machine sliding about. Unless you have a very firm, free-standing table, you must either buy a special table or ask a handyman to make you a shelf-table fixed to the wall. This must be very strong, with legs as well as brackets. On the whole I prefer a free-standing table, because I use a lot of coned yarn and the longer the run between cone and machine, the smoother the knitting seems to be. But it is a matter of choice.

Your tools must be handy — and this includes the tools that come with the machine and anything else (note book, pencil etc that you use regularly).

Finally you should *wear something suitable* for knitting. This sounds ridiculous, but in fact the wrong clothes can cause small disasters: loose sleeves, floppy bows, loosely knitted or woven fabrics, fringes, beads — all these can catch on the needles as you lean across your machine.

If possible, keep your sewing machine and sewing accessories in the same place as your knitting machine. Knitting, in the conventional sense of producing shaped garments, is only part of what you will be doing, once you become expert. Your knitting machine is a wonderful appliance that will *make fabric*, either shaped as you knit or made in lengths and then treated like bought fabric, to make a wide variety of clothing and home furnishings.

Fair isle windcheaters knitted on a double bed machine with automatic colour changer. This particular stitch — which takes a fine yarn and turns it into a sturdy, warm and hard wearing fabric — can be done only with two beds. But there are other 'thickening' stitches, some of which can be knitted on a single bed machine.

6
Let's Start Knitting

It is human nature — when you are starting on something as exciting as machine knitting — to look through the pattern books, choose a really elegant suit or evening dress, and decide to dazzle family and friends by making this at your first attempt. But most of us make better progress if we start with something simple.

I am assuming you will already have done a good many practice pieces. And once you have mastered the operation of your machine, there is no reason why even these should not be turned into something useful.

Consider the things that you can make with just squares or rectangles of knitting:

Scarves

are straight pieces of fabric, usually fringed at the ends.

Tension is not vital (it doesn't matter if they are slightly longer, shorter, narrower or wider) but you are learning, not just making scarves, so follow the instructions for making tension squares and try to make your scarves come up exactly to the size you have decided on.

Your first scarf can be in a plain colour. Press it, sew it up, fringe it — and you should have a very nice scarf, for very much less than shop price.

Now let's try some variations:
add stripes — these can be school or club colours, or bands of fair isle;
knit your scarf in two separate lengths, in different colours. Join these together and you have a reversible scarf — one side, say, brown and the other beige. You can knit the 'outside' of your scarf in a fair isle or tuck or slip or weaving stitch, and the 'inside' in plain knitting. This is where the tension square becomes vital: the two halves must measure the same,

but if you use a stitch pattern for one, and plain stocking stitch for the other, the number of rows and stitches to the inch is unlikely to be the same.

You can line a stole with bought fabric — silk or satin for an evening stole, soft jersey or 'bush baby' type fabric for a more homely stole to keep you warm.

If you have a machine that does single motif work (and if you can afford it, I think they are well worth the money) now is the time to swank a little. A black stole with a single silver rose at one end is glamorous. A brilliant red scarf with a yellow racing car at one end, and a bright green one at the other end, will please a young wearer. And my own favourite is a pale blue scarf, with a yellow teddy bear at one end. Teddy holds a string from which balloons seem to have come adrift, because they are floating up-up-up towards the other end of the scarf — a red one, a green one, a royal blue one, an orange one . . . A knitting machine is not only useful. It's fun.

By now you have probably kitted out the whole family with scarves. I know of some knitters who have never got beyond scarves — but not because they are unsuccessful. One man makes only scarves and stoles, which he sells in a market, and does very nicely. Several women are making steady spare-time incomes from school and club scarves.

But most knitters want to go on, until they can knit anything that's knittable. So let's think of some more easy shapes:

Cushion Covers

are just as easy as scarves. They can be made in stripes, in random yarn, or each side can be knitted in two halves, changing colour halfway, to give a giant check effect, like this:

Red	Blue
Yellow	Black

A button — or better still a pompom — where the colours meet, looks good.

The shapes are easy. Squares and rectangles need no explanation. If you wish to make a bolster shape, you can simply gather the ends and

THIS IS LUXURY knitting — needs a modern punch card machine like the Knitmaster 326. But even with a simple machine, you can make a dress with graceful, simple lines like this — and then add interest in many ways.

finish off with a big tassel or pompom. If you want circular ends and don't feel up to the partial knitting which these involve, you can crochet the circles (double crochet, in rounds) or you can knit squares of a suitable size, back them with interfacing (iron-on for wool) mark out the circle you need, machine round this (if you have a swing needle machine use one row of medium length straight stitching, one row of medium length, medium width zig-zag stitch; if you have only a straight-stitch machine, then two rows of straight stitching). In either case, use a thread such as Drima or Gutermann's, which I find good for stitching up woollies. Cut away the surplus, then machine the ends to the tube, right sides facing.

This is your very first attempt at 'cut and sew' — the technique which in my view opens up a new world to the machine knitter. If you feel like being a little more adventurous, knit some plain (or striped, or suitably patterned) squares or rectangles, back them with interfacing, draw (on to the interfacing) some very simple shapes, machine round these shapes, cut out, join together, and you have fun cushions. If you prefer you can join the two sides together before you cut away the surplus.

You need not be an artist to draw these shapes. I am thinking of something as simple as this:

you can make a crochet circle, or a pompom, for the centre, you can embroider stamens, or outline the separate petals with chain stitch.

you can tie a bow round his neck. You can knit him a cord tail (or crochet or twist one). You can embroider features and whiskers — even a hint of paws. You can knit him a much thicker tail, stuff this firmly, and use him as a draught excluder.

You could also make a simple Teddy Bear shape — give him a bow tie or a muffler, embroider his features. You could knit from his feet to his waist in one colour (for trousers), and add braces to go over his shoulders, or a bib and braces. In the same way you can make a doll, a golliwog, or a clown.

You can make a 'cuddle skirt', either in one long piece (knitted sideways) or by joining strips or squares. (A 'cuddle skirt' is fairly full, not shaped, but gathered in to the waist, rather like a dirndl.)

A skirt like this is very easy to knit, is useful, warm and good looking, and lends itself to all sorts of ideas. You can make it in random or planned stripes, you can introduce a band or bands of fair isle or weaving. You can dot it with single motifs, add embroidery or Swiss darning. You can trim it with braid (knitted or bought) or fringe, or bobbles; you can line it (leave the lining loose — catching it only at the waist). You can make it short enough for country walks, or long and glamorous for evening wear.

This chapter could go on and on — there are so many attractive things you can make from simple shapes. But by now, I hope you have gained confidence and are longing to launch out on your own. It is much more satisfying to put your own ideas into practice than to follow someone else's suggestions.

We are now ready to go on to something with more shaping in it. I am well aware that some of you will be way ahead of me — probably making really elegant clothes by this time. But this book aims to help the knitter who — at first — is not too confident about machine knitting.

Your instruction book should tell you all you need to know about the actual process of knitting — how to increase and decrease, shape necklines and shoulders — and you should study these instructions really carefully, and practise them, several times, before you make your first garment.

Remember to make a tension square — and make it carefully. Even the simplest sleeveless tank top cannot be right if the tension is wrong.

If, when you are making your first garment, you run into trouble, it could be that you are:

not taking enough trouble to get your tension right (see Chapter Eleven);

using unsuitable yarn (a pattern designed for a firm crêpe will not knit up the same in a soft baby yarn);

having casting-on troubles, or losing stitches (turn back to Chapter Two);

having difficulty with things like bands, collars etc — if necessary, take an advance look at Chapter Fourteen.

spoiling your work with poor making up (see Chapter Eight).

Just a few words about choosing your first pattern: many beginners start with a baby garment (even if they have no baby in the family to knit for). They think it will be easier. I am not sure this is right. Tiny garments are 'fiddly' — I consider it is easier to make an adult garment. If by chance you do not have the simple, plain garment that you want in a pattern especially designed for your machine, look in

Patons' Simple Machine Knits — No 194

this gives a classic pattern for a sweater with a set-in sleeve in Patons' Purple Heather 4-ply — a lovely trouble-free wool. Sizes go from 32″ (80 cm) to 38″ (95 cm) and the tension is a nice easy one of 7 stitches and 10 rows to the inch. In the same book there is a pattern for a raglan cardigan — same wool, same tension — in sizes 32″ (80 cm) to 40″ (100 cm) (you can omit the stripes if you wish).

Also in

Patons' Machine Knits No 3 — 181

you will find a sweater and sleeveless cardigan, sizes 38″ (95 cm) to 44″ (110 cm) in Patons' FIONA — which is one of the nicest yarns it is possible to knit with.

These books are obtainable from good woolshops; in case of difficulty write to Patons & Baldwins.

Of course, you need not use these patterns or these yarns. But if you are in doubt, these are good garments (and good yarns) to use as a jumping off ground. One of these garments, in one of the sizes, is pretty sure to come in handy for someone in your family. You can use the pattern(s) several times if you wish (I know some knitters who have used them hundreds of times!) altering the length, adding stripes or bands of fair isle etc.

Once you reach the stage where your finished work is good, your next ambition will probably be to turn out a lot of knitting, on your machine, in the shortest possible time.

The next chapter gives you some time-savers.

7
Speeding up

Machine knitting is a quick and easy way of producing garments. Experienced knitters are always trying to find ways of making it even quicker — but experience takes time. So here, in the hope that they will help new knitters, are some of the time-savers that I have discovered for myself, or learned from other knitters.

But first — DON'T try to speed up by operating the machine faster. It is best to work at a steady, rhythmic speed. Beginners — finding how easy it is — sometimes get quite carried away. The cam box whizzes to and fro at ever increasing speed and suddenly all the stitches are off, or the yarn has run out, or some other disaster has struck. And the beginner is not equipped to deal with these small tragedies. The experienced knitter simply puts the stitches back on to the needles, removes the cam box, re-sets the pattern panel, unravels the yarn — in short, she copes with small disasters almost without thinking what she is doing. Beginners do not have this confidence or know-how. And since confidence is an important part of successful knitting, it is much better to work at a moderate pace and avoid disaster.

But there are many timesavers that the beginner can use.

Raglan Shaping

If you make a garment with raglan sleeves, you will have to decrease (fully fashioned) a number of times — on both sides of each of four sections: back, front, two sleeves.

Very often a pattern tells you to decrease one stitch every — say — two or four rows. Let us assume your pattern tells you to decrease one stitch each end, every four rows, twenty times. This means you will have to make forty fully fashioned decreases — and each decrease takes time. Why not cut the number of decreases down to half? You can do this by decreasing twice as many stitches (in this case two stitches each end) half as many times (in this case ten times) so you must knit eight rows, between decreases, instead of four. Some knitters claim they save at least half an hour on a garment by shaping in this way.

This kind of decreasing looks good, too, as well as saving time. Some of you will find instructions for this kind of decrease in your instruction book, but for the benefit of other knitters:

> Take the triple transfer tool, lift the stitches off the 1st, 2nd and 3rd needles on the right hand side. Place these stitches on to the 3rd, 4th and 5th needles. There will be 2 stitches on the 5th needle and 2 stitches on the 4th needle, with 2 empty needles at the edge. Put these empty needles back into non-working position. Do the same at the other end.

When you become more proficient you can be more adventurous and work with the 5-decker tool (if your machine provides one). Or you can use the double decker tool and move the stitches from the 3rd and 4th needles on to the 5th and 6th needles, then the 1st and 2nd stitches on to the 3rd and 4th needles. Needles 1 and 2 will now be empty and should be pushed back into non-working position.

The advantage of making the decrease further in is that it will be more clearly visible, after the sections are joined together, and as fully fashioned shaping gives a garment a look of quality, this is usually an advantage.

However, fully fashioned shaping — even if you cut the number of decreases down to half — takes time. *It is well worth it* if you are making a good quality garment that will be worn when the wearer wishes to look elegant. Is it worth it when you are making a play sweater for a little boy who will probably fall straight into a puddle, or climb a tree? Only you can decide this. Even if you are a stickler for perfection — and the best knitters are — remember that in some stitch patterns — and this includes all-over fair isle, which is delightful for children's play clothes — fully fashioned shaping scarcely shows. Nor does it show — except in absolutely plain, top quality fine-knits — in underarm sleeve seams, side seams and set-in sleeve shaping. When you have joined these pieces together (*if* you do this properly) fully fashioned shaping is barely noticeable and can be cut out if you are short of time.

Increasing is sometimes quicker than decreasing — not the fully fashioned increase, which is sometimes necessary for good appearance on a collar or neck band, but the simple increase which is made by pushing one more needle into working position. So if you can increase, instead of decrease, you will save time. You can do this by starting at the top and working downwards, on a raglan shape (if fully fashioned shaping is not necessary). I have heard knitters claim that they save as much as an hour on a garment, by doing this.

Shaping the Head of a Sleeve

also takes time, because of the casting off and the decreasing. Try shaping by putting the needles into holding position:

Say your pattern tells you to cast off 7 stitches at the beginning of the next 2 rows, 5 stitches at the beginning of the next 2 rows, 3 stitches at the beginning of the next 2 rows and so on.

Set your machine so that needles placed in holding position will not knit down. Then, instead of decreasing 7 stitches, with the cam box on the right, put 7 stitches at the left into holding position. Knit the row, take the yarn round the first needle in holding position (this prevents a hole forming), put seven stitches on the right side into holding position, knit the row, take the yarn round the first needle in holding position, put 5 stitches at the left into holding position . . . and so on.

When you have finished shaping the sleeve head, knit one row — at a much looser tension (approx. three stitch sizes larger) over all the stitches, knit several rows with waste yarn and strip off. This not only saves a lot of time, it makes a nice smooth curve at the top of the sleeve — easy to sew up.

Some knitters like to take a knitting needle of suitable size and cast off by hand, because in this way they can make a very loose cast-off (and it does not take long). But other knitters simply run the yarn through the last row of stitches knitted in main yarn; they fasten the end of the yarn into the seam after the sleeve has been sewn in.

When shaping in this way, knitters sometimes complain that the stitches come off the needles in working position. This can be avoided by hanging small weights (a few rows down) just below the last few needles in working position, on either side. Move these weights up — and in — as necessary. The stitches are then lightly held down on the needles.

Some knitters use this method of shaping for raglan, as well as set-in sleeves.

Shaping by putting into holding position, rather than decreasing or casting off, can be made even faster: it is necessary for the yarn to go under the first needle in holding position (to avoid a hole). This means picking up the yarn, and slipping it under the needle, on every row. Try this, and see if it is quicker:

If you need to put 7 needles into holding position on the left (the cam box will be at the right) push 6 needles into holding position on the left, knit across (cam box on the left) push one more needle into holding position (making 7). Then, as you knit across, the yarn will wrap itself round this last needle.

Casting Off

---

is a time-consumer. In my opinion it is the only operation that is not considerably quicker with a knitting machine (though practised knitters do sometimes work up a great speed). Fortunately it is often possible to omit the casting off altogether: instead you simply knit a few rows with waste yarn (I find seven a good number) and strip the work off the machine. (For the benefit of knitters with older type machines, whose instruction books may not make it clear what 'stripping off' means, this means running the cam box across the needles without yarn. As there is no yarn to make stitches, the loops already on the needle will simply slide off and the work is removed from the machine.)

Imagine you are knitting the back of a simple sweater. You have 100 stitches; you know that each shoulder will have 32 stitches, and the back neck will have 36.

The pattern tells you to shape the shoulders by casting off 8 stitches 8 times (i.e. 4 8-stitch decreases each end).

Instead of doing this, put the needles into holding position — just as I explained for shaping the sleeve head. Then, when you have 32 stitches in holding position at each end, break off the main yarn, take a small ball of contrast wool, knit several rows over the 36 stitches still in working position, and strip off. Put the 36 needles back into non-working position. The back neck stitches are now held (they cannot run) until you are ready for them. If you wish to pick them up to knit the neckband, it is easy to do so. If you wish to conceal the neck edge completely, inside the neckband (which I think is the best way), you can run a length of yarn through the last row of the back neck, and then either pick up one row further down, or knit the neckband separately and sew it on. In either case *you need not cast off.*

Following the instructions in your book, push the 32 needles nearest the cam box back into working position and with main yarn knit one row over the 32 stitches. You do not need to knit this row at a larger tension (as you did for the sleeve head, as the shoulder needs to be firm, not stretchy). Knit a few rows with waste yarn, and strip off.

Put the empty needles back into non-working position, and then knit the second shoulder in the same way.

You have not cast off, but the stitches are being held, so you can now do what is necessary to complete shoulders and back neck.

You can join the shoulders either by grafting — which is invisible if properly done, and with a little practice can be done quite quickly — or by replacing the stitches on the needles, right sides of work facing, (each needle will have two stitches on it) knit one row, and cast off. You have had to cast off, but only once for each shoulder instead of twice. Some knitters prefer to knit one stitch through the other, before casting off.

When you come to the front of the garment, you can shape the neckline with the holding position — some knitters like to cast off the centre section, and then use the holding position for the rest of the shaping. But you need not cast off — you can simply run a thread through the stitches, tie the ends of the thread together, and slide the needles out of these stitches. Put the empty needles back into non-working position.

You will come across other occasions when you can avoid casting off. Whenever a pattern tells you to cast off, stop and think: it may not be necessary.

Casting Off in Fair Isle

---

worries a good many knitters. If you use just one yarn, the other is left behind and is not in position for the next row. If you use both yarns, the cast-off is bulky. Casting off alternate stitches with background and trimming colour is neat, but takes rather a long time. I find the easiest way is always to cast off on the side furthest away from the lock, using a separate length of yarn.

When Knitting a Hem

---

with a closed edge cast-on, you can save time by casting on over alternate needles (bring the other needles up into working position on the second row). This means you will have half as many loops to lift on to the needles, and you will have to wind the wool round the needles (to cast on) only half as many times. As every alternate needle will hold only one stitch (as you close the hem) the join will be less bulky, too, which is another advantage.

You should also consider using adhesive hemming web, (see Chapter Sixteen) and ironing your hem into position, rather than lifting the loops or sewing by hand. You can of course use it only on a yarn that can be pressed according to the maker's instructions (for the hemming web). You can find these adhesive webs on good haberdashery counters.

Stitching Up the Hem Section

of the side seam of a garment is trying. Beginners sometimes stitch through four thicknesses, which is very ugly. The alternative is to stitch carefully first on the outside then on the inside, which takes time (and does not always look perfect).

Save time — and improve the appearance — by leaving about three stitches each end free — that is, do not lift the loops on to the needles, when you close the hem. Leaving these ends free means that you can sew up in one straight line — right from the armhole to the bottom of the garment. If you make up by machine (which in my view is the realistic way to make up machine knitting) you can simply machine right to the very end.

If you want to make a ribbed or mock rib welt, and still be able to machine stitch all the way down, you should work the last few stitches each end in plain stocking stitch. It is difficult to make a neat job of sewing ribs by machine.

This advice applies to the closed-edged cast-on. If you have cast on with waste yarn, you can still leave the first few loops each end free — simply run a thread (something that can be easily pulled out later) through these open loops, to stop them from running. When your side seam is completed, press these stitches, and catch them down invisibly, removing the thread.

When Knitting Long Sections

such as trouser legs, skirt panels, front and back of sweaters etc, you can save time in the making up by putting a marker thread every — say — fifty rows. You then have several points to match up, so that pinning the seams together is quicker and easier.

Complicated Shapings

can often be simplified — which saves time. I was recently knitting a number of tank tops for quite small children. The armhole struck me as unnecessarily complicated. I looked at the diagram, saw how many stitches would have to be decreased in all, cast off one block of 5 stitches, then did single decreases, on alternate rows, until I had the required number of stitches left. This was much quicker than the original pattern (I timed it with another knitter) and looked just as good.

Shoulder shapings are often, in my opinion, unnecessarily gradual. If you need to cast off 40 stitches, some pattern writers tend to give this as 10 decreases of 4 stitches each: for simple casual clothes I would be more inclined to do 4 decreases of 10 stitches each. This is perhaps rather an extreme example, but I almost always simplify the shoulder shaping by reducing the number of steps, and I can never see that my garments look less professional than those knitted according to the pattern. In very expensive yarn, for top quality garments, I would follow the experts (just to be on the safe side) but for everyday, run-of-the-mill knitting I think that the *experienced* knitter is justified in taking some short cuts.

Another time saver, when making garments for children, is to knit *front(s) and back in one*, as far as the armholes. Then, if it is a cardigan, you divide your work into three.

For example, if you have 160 stitches on the machine, take 40 for one front, 80 for the back, 40 for the second front. If it is a sweater, you divide the stitches in half. This of course is only possible if the total number of stitches needed is not more than the number of needles on your machine. Knitting this way cuts out one seam for a sweater, two for a cardigan. And as it is quicker to knit one wide piece of knitting than to knit two or three narrow ones, you save time in this way too.

(Knitters with double bed machines can knit sweaters (to the armholes) sleeves (to the cap) and trousers (to the crutch) in circular knitting. When you reach the armholes, sleeve cap, or crutch, you must change to single bed stocking stitch or to half-tubular, with an opening on one side).

Stitching Bands

to the fronts of cardigans is a fairly lengthy job. Some knitters prefer to knit the front, cast on the number of stitches required for the band, and then join the band to the front as they knit, by picking up the edge stitch of the front and placing it on to the end needle being used for the band. I do not find this a real timesaver, but so many knitters recommend it that I think it fair to pass on the hint. I attach bands fairly fast with a combination of these methods:

I put cardigans on a dressmaker's dummy and pin the bands in position — I find this much quicker than trying to do the job on a table. I leave the garment on the dummy for a few hours, in case it drops.

For many years, I used to mattress stitch bands to the fronts, by hand. This was a very slow job at first, although I got much quicker (and better) with practice. I then used to slip stitch the band to the inside, using matching sewing thread, which I find easier and neater than using the knitting yarn.

But for some time now I have been machine stitching bands to fronts. This is much quicker *and* it gives a beautiful finish when you are proficient at it. Your first few attempts may be poor — I remember mine were very disappointing — but keep practising, on odd swatches of knitting, and you will get better and better (see Chapter Eight).

Waste Yarn

is a great time-saver, when starting and finishing work. But it is not necessary to cast on with waste yarn every single time you want to start a garment. I keep three pieces of waste knitting — one over all the needles, one over 100 needles, one (for bands) over 30 needles, and just hook up the required number of stitches on to the needles. (You need not be too careful about getting a straight line.) I work one row with casting-on cord (I like to do this from left to right, so that I have the cam box on the right to start knitting properly). Continue knitting in main yarn. When the casting-on cord is pulled out, the waste knitting will fall away.

Coned Yarn

saves time: you knit from one long length, and the yarn you can buy on cones usually does not need waxing. This means you cut out the task of winding and waxing. It also means no loose ends to darn in when you have completed your knitting.

Coned Shetland, however, needs to be washed before it is made up — which nullifies some of the time-saving property.

Darning In Loose Ends

takes time, especially if you thread each one into a needle. I find it much quicker to use the latchet tool supplied with most machines — and some knitters 'darn in' as they go, by lifting the loose ends over the edge needle for five or six rows. This works well with fine to medium yarn but — because both ends are 'darned in' in the same direction — it may make the side seam rather bulky in a thicker yarn. Knitters who regularly make up on the sewing machine often simply cut loose ends off, leaving about an inch. This would not do for really top quality knitwear, but for everyday garments it seems to me quite satisfactory. Don't cut the ends short until after the garment has been securely machined together — the machine stitching makes it virtually impossible for the loose end to pull out.

With single bed work I think it is better to darn loose ends into the side seam, where they should be invisible. With double bed work it is sometimes possible to darn in — on the wrong side — in such a way that it is quite invisible from the right side.

Winding and Waxing

(when you are not using coned yarns) can be speeded up if you do all the wool for a garment at one time. If this makes your arm ache too much (we badly need a neat, small, not-too-expensive electric wool-winder, in my view), then try to do it in not more than two or three sessions. Stopping every few minutes to wind another ball of wool slows down your knitting considerably.

Weighing Oddments

of yarn, before you put them into your stock, can save a good deal of time. If you have just one huge muddle of small quantities, you will have to check every time you wish to use some of them — is there enough of that bright red to go with the navy etc? If — when you find you have small quantities left over — you weigh the yarn, put it in a see-through plastic bag with a note pinned to it giving ply and quantity, you can quickly sort out what you need.

A Tidy Workroom

is a great time-saver. Make sure that tools and other vital accessories are *never* taken away — a whole knitting session can be wasted hunting for something that ought to be permanently with your machine. It saves time to have a quick clean-up every time you finish a knitting session: I like to run the crevice tool of a small vacuum cleaner over my machine, to remove all fluff and dust, then wipe with a clean cloth. Oil regularly (see your instruction book). A dirty, clogged up machine, that needs oil, is a time-waster — AND takes a lot of the pleasure out of knitting. And NEVER TAKE FOOD OR DRINK into your knitting room. It is tempting, when you are trying to finish something, to work as you drink your tea or coffee, or eat a quick sandwich. But one careless move can tip your drink over your knitting (which will have to be redone) and into the machine (which may have to be stripped down), and crumbs and blobs of butter can also do a lot of damage.

Keeping Notes

can save a lot of time. Whenever you do something, in knitting, that is not absolutely in accordance with a pattern, you should write down exactly where you differed from the pattern, and how. Even if you knit strictly according to pattern, make a note of the number of the pattern and where to find it, whenever you make a garment that you are likely to want to make again. While you are still fairly new to machine knitting, the more information about your work you can write down the better: keep a note of how long it takes to knit a garment (later, when you may want to take orders, this helps you to fix a fair price); keep a note of how much wool each section of a garment takes — if you want to use that pattern again, but perhaps making the front or the sleeves in a contrast colour, you won't have to guess whether you have enough yarn; make a note of the iron setting that made a good job of the pressing for a particular yarn; of the sewing machine settings that did a good job of the stitching up. Keep notes about the cost of the garments you knit — if, later, you want to take orders this will be a helpful guide. Even if you do not wish to make money with your machine, you may — as many knitters do — like to keep a note of everything you spend on yarn etc and compare this with what you would have paid in the shops for similar knitwear. This gives you a clear picture of what your knitting machine saves you.

As you become more proficient, you will discover all kinds of interesting possibilities. You will be so pleased when you make a discovery, that you may feel sure you will never forget it — but you will, by the time you have done a good deal more knitting and probably had a good many more bright ideas. SO WRITE IT DOWN, where you can find it to use again and again. For example, if you have a punch card machine you may not yet realise in how very many ways most of the punch cards can be used. The Knitmaster 321/3 instruction book gives some examples of variations on punch card patterns — but you may find many more, which means you are adding to your collection of stitch patterns without having to buy or punch new cards.

Don't keep notes on odd pieces of paper — even if you do not lose them, you will waste time hunting madly through them to find the particular note you need. Buy a big, inexpensive exercise book (or if you like to type your notes, you may find a scrap book ideal). If you do not wish to spend money on a special book, save all leaflets etc with printing on only one side, suitable wrapping paper — in fact any oddments of paper that you can write on, and either staple them together or stitch them with the sewing machine. Try to separate, in some way, the different types of notes — patterns, punch card variations, iron or sewing machine settings etc. And of course you must keep your tension notes, most carefully (see Chapter Eleven): they will save you time again and again.

Don't Waste the Time

---

you spend actually at your machine. Darning in ends and hand-finishing can be done when you are sitting with the rest of the family or listening to radio or television, or talking to friends. Most husbands complain that their wives spend too much time at their machines, anyway, so there is no sense in sitting — alone — doing hand jobs that could easily be done in the living room.

Repetition Makes For Speed

If I have a number of identical (or even very similar) garments to make, I do all the backs, then all the fronts, then all the sleeves . . . I am sure that I save time this way: I seem to speed up, and find that by the third or fourth time I knit a section, I save about ten minutes on my original time. I also like to do darning in, hand-finishing, washing, pressing, making up etc in big batches. Apart from the fact that I speed up, when I do the same thing several times, it also means getting out the necessary equipment only once instead of a number of times.

Limiting Your Range of Yarns

is a good time-saver. If you limit yourself to just one yarn, then you can quickly make tension swatches of all the stitch patterns you want to use. Even if you use two or three different yarns, you can still make all the tension squares you are likely to need in one big session, and from then on you can use these tension squares for all the garments you wish to knit. However, this has disadvantages too. If you design your own patterns, or use a Knit Radar or Knit Leader, you can (within reasonable limits) knit the garment of your choice in the tension that best suits your yarn. But if you always follow printed patterns, then you will find that your limited range of tensions makes many patterns unsuitable for you. Secondly, if you limit yourself to just one (or even two or three) yarns, you miss a lot of the creative fun of machine knitting — trying out new yarns and combinations of yarns, taking advantage of bargains etc. A good many knitters compromise: for their regular work they stick to one or two yarns, but they leave some time for experimenting and improvising.

There are four major time-savers, for the machine knitter, that I shall be dealing with in later chapters. These are:

Making up on the sewing machine — See Chapter Eight.

The Cut-and-Sew Method — See Chapter Nine.
Dressmaking Aids and Accessories — See Chapter Sixteen.
The Pattern Tracing Devices (such as Knit Radar and Knit Leader) — See Chapter Twelve.

Some knitters work fairly quickly, until they come to a particular item which causes them trouble — perhaps pockets, or buttonholes. I have tried to deal with some of these in Chapter Fourteen. (*Is this your Problem?*)

This present chapter — with the other chapters that I have referred knitters to — should save beginners quite a lot of time. But nothing will take the place of practice and experience. If, right at the beginning of your machine knitting, you start to feel downhearted and wonder whether it really is going to be as quick as you hoped, stop and remember how it was with other skills you have acquired: the competent driver once dithered and panicked every time she found herself in a line of traffic; the fast typist once fumbled for the right keys; the keen reader once had to stop and think which letter represented which sound . . . and that's how it will be with machine knitting (which takes *much less time* to learn than either driving, typing or reading). Just at first, it will seem strange. Quite soon it will seem easy. Before long you will be really proficient — if you keep knitting.

There's nothing fuddy-duddy about today's machine knitting. When the Knitmaster 326 was launched, with a fashion show, most of us sat and gaped — one way-out, stunning, fascinating garment appeared after the other. Of course you can be as restrained as you like — plain classics are always in demand — but with young people in the family, or when you want to make something startling to bring yourself to the notice of boutiques or private customers, remember you can really hit the heights of fashion with a knitting machine.

8
Making up your Knitting

Your knitting machine, properly used, will produce beautiful fabric. This is very little use unless you can turn that beautiful fabric into beautiful garments.

Many of you will think this too obvious to be mentioned. But unfortunately it is not obvious to a good many knitters. I quite often meet knitters who complain that their knitting 'never really looks right' and as soon as I see it I know why: they have not taken the trouble to make it up properly. But these knitters would take great care with the making up of a fabric — perhaps much less attractive — that they had bought in a shop.

Recently I had to examine work done by about thirty machine knitters who wanted to earn some money by knitting. Less than half a dozen of them had produced anything saleable. In every case the *knitting* was good (the machine took care of that) but when it came to the making up, I saw some sorry sights:

Seams clumsily oversewn; shoulders joined in jagged 'steps' with the cast-off edge showing; neckbands picked up so as to leave gaps and holes; a neck band sewn to a pink sweater with yellow wool (!); raglan seams roughly cobbled up; cardigan bands too tight on one side and too loose on the other — these are not exaggerations, but truthful examples of what I saw.

All these people wanted to earn by knitting; all of them could knit. It was only the making-up that defeated them. I wished so much that all those knitters lived near to me, so that we could get together over a cup of tea and sort out the problems. I am hoping that at least some of them may read this book, decide to master the making-up, and become successful knitters.

There is nothing mysterious or difficult about making up machine-knitted garments — nothing that you and I cannot learn to do quite quickly, once we have been shown how, and spent a little time practising. And yet I have known people to put their machines away, and give up the idea of knitting, because they could not make a good job of putting the knitted pieces together. Let's see what we can do about this.

Let's begin by completely forgetting the ways we may have been taught when we first started to knit (by hand). Most of us were taught to oversew the seams. In my view this looks bad even on hand knitting; on machine knitting it is a disaster. Occasionally I see tiny baby clothes, in a fancy stitch pattern and a very soft wool, oversewn so neatly that the effect is quite good. But this is a very special case — and I still think the job could have been done better and faster with other methods.

There are several ways of making up machine knitted garments:

(1) *a neat strong back stitch.* Can be acceptable, if really well done.

(2) *mattress stitch.* This is the perfect way, for quality garments — and particularly for raglan shaping (see diagram).

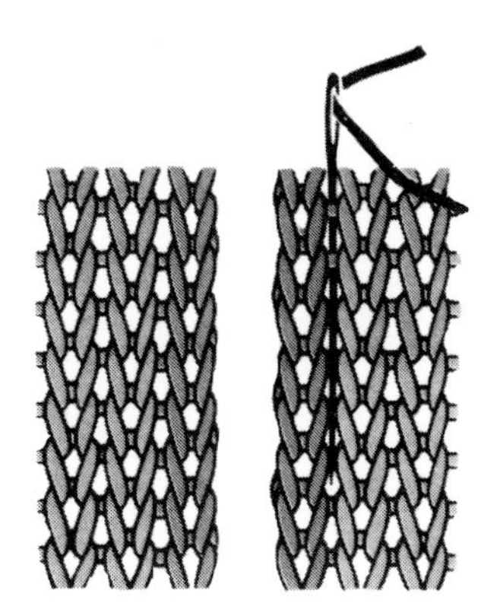

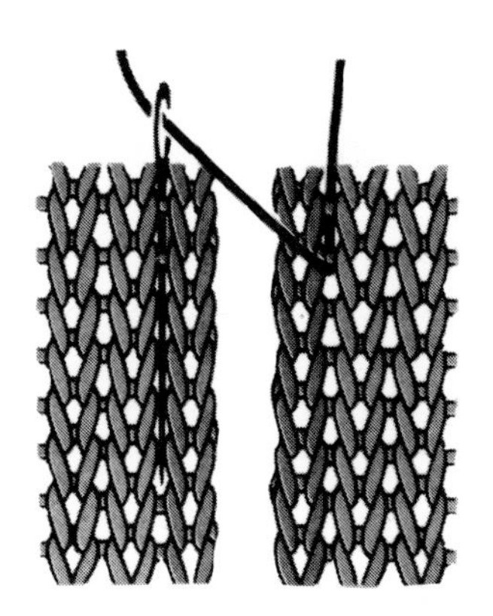

1. Thread a tapestry needle with knitting yarn.
2. Take the bars of the first 2 rows on the side of the edge stitch and pull through.
3. Take the bars of 2 rows next to the edge stitch of the second piece, as shown in second diagram.

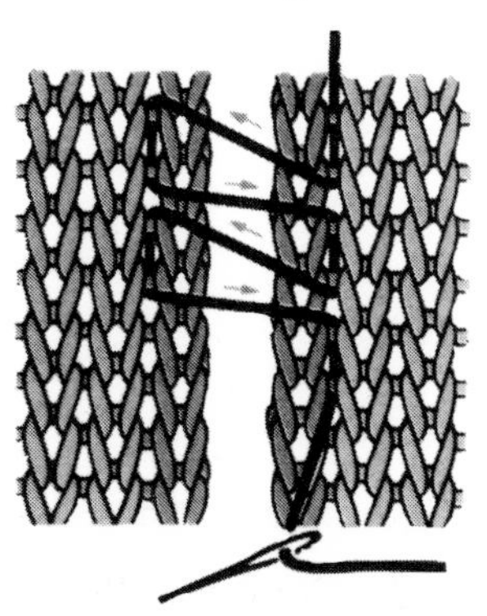

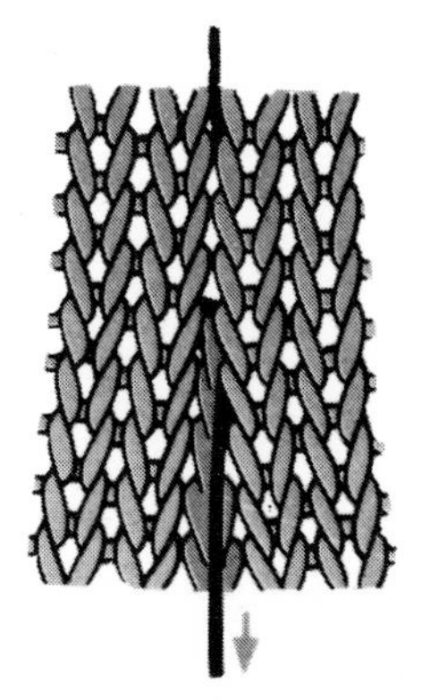

4. Continue taking 2 bars next to the edge stitch on alternate sides 2 or 3 times.
5. Hold the fabric on the wrong side by the seam and pull the sewing thread tight, this will close up the stitches and leave an invisible seam on the right side.

(3) *making up on the sewing machine.*
For the woman who wants to make money with her machine, for the woman who knits for a large family, for the woman with very limited spare time, who still wants to turn out a good many garments on her knitting machine, I have no doubt at all that this is the answer. A very good answer too — garments made up on the sewing machine can look professional and stand up to hard wear. There will be finishing touches that are best done by hand, but if the main seams are machine-stitched, the saving in time will be enormous (as much as 2 hours on a garment) and in most cases the results will be at least as good as hand sewing.

But although so many knitters are now making up on the sewing machine — or wishing they could — there is very little advice about how to do it. Exceptions are Mary Weaver's books (see Chapter Twelve). But these books deal with specific machines; unless you have one of those machines you will be unlikely to have the book. I want to show owners of *any* knitting machine how to make up on the sewing machine, quickly and well.

I do most of my sewing up on a Jones Automatic — it is one of the medium priced machines (my model is several years old); some of the latest (and most expensive!) sewing machines have special stitches for sewing up knits, and these make the job even easier. But I manage very well on my not-too-new, not-too-expensive model, and I know knitters who have even simpler machines, and can still do an excellent job. It is a great advantage to have a swing-needle machine, but even a straight-stitch machine can be used, as long as this is an electric or a treadle. I think it would be difficult to work with a hand machine, as I always need both my hands when stitching up knitwear. However, I have no doubt it could be done, on a hand machine, but it would be much slower.

I use a very narrow zig-zag stitch — so narrow that it is quite safe to use the straight sewing foot. The settings for my machine are swing ½, length 3¼; I use a very light pressure — on my machine it is between 'silk' and 'cotton'. I use the zipper foot, and position this so that the edge of the knitting curls over it as I stitch: I find this gives a seam of just the right width — not wide and clumsy, yet not too near the edge. You must use a good quality thread that will not break in wear; a rough cheap cotton is a false economy. I like either Drima or Gutermann's 100% polyester thread.

Before starting to machine, I pin the two pieces of knitting together, with pins at right angles to the edges. And although my machine will easily sew over pins, I work quite slowly and remove them as I go. This means I can check, every few inches, to make sure that the edges are even and that the piece underneath has not slipped over to the left, where the needle would miss it. If I have left the last few stitches of the hem free (see Chapter Seven 'Stitching up the hem section') I can machine right to the end of the seam. I think it is a mistake to try to machine two thicknesses of ribbing, so I either finish the ribbing by hand, or (when knitting) I leave the last few stitches at each end in plain stocking stitch.

Now let's do some making up together.

Imagine you have knitted several garments — cardigans, sweaters, dresses etc. Now you want to make them up, as professionally *and as quickly* as possible.

Darn in any odd ends.

Whenever you finish a piece of knitting, and remove it from the machine, you should hold it firmly top and bottom and pull it lengthwise. Then look carefully to make sure there are no dropped stitches or other faults. I am not expecting faults, but there is always the possibility of a poor section of yarn that breaks or frays, or a knot that slipped by, so much better check each piece of knitting as it comes off the machine. If you forgot to do this, do it now.

Hand-wash any pieces that need washing (e.g. oiled Shetland). Spin dry (*very* short spin for synthetics), rinse, (add fabric softener if wished) and spin again. Heavy knitteds should be dried flat on towels or on a special drying rack. Lightweight ones, as long as the fabric is firm, may be hung over a rail that is covered with a clean towel — but only after being partially dried in the spinner or between towels.

While you are waiting for these to dry, press any pieces that did not need washing, being careful with synthetics. With wool I like to use a fairly hot iron and very damp cloth. Synthetics need great care. If you buy a branded synthetic, follow the spinners' recommendations absolutely. If you buy oddments on cones, then try pressing a small test piece — use a cool iron and a dry cloth and probably you will find this gives good results. If you are not satisfied, then experiment with more heat — but be sure you are using only a small expendable piece of knitting. Some synthetics are so soft, or so crunchy, that they look splendid without any pressing at all.

Do not press ribbing, or any raised stitch. You will flatten it out and spoil it. If you want to, you can pin it out, cover it with a damp cloth and leave it to dry — but this is not often necessary. Or if it is pure wool, you can cover with a damp cloth and hold the iron close enough to cause steam to rise from the cloth, without letting the iron actually touch the cloth. Try this out on a spare piece of knitting first.

When the washed pieces are dry, they too should be pressed, in the appropriate way.

Really warm and practical, but eye-catching too. Collar, cuffs and welts are in 'real' ribbing, on a ribbing attachment or double bed machine, but those with only single bed machines could substitute mock or Continental rib. This neat, all-over fair isle design is typical of many available on punch cards or in chart form, — or it is not difficult to work out your own designs. Because the yarn not in use is looped behind the knitted stitches, this type of knitting can produce a warm, sturdy garment from a fine yarn. This is made by a comparative beginner.

Next, do any cut-and-sew necklines (see Chapter Nine).

Then, if there are pocket tops or other small items that need hand-finishing, deal with them, because it is easier to handle the separate pieces than the made-up garment.

Next — if your garment has set-in sleeves — look at the shoulders.

If the garment is in stocking stitch, in a double knit, 4-ply or firm 3-ply, then I like to graft the two sets of stitches together (I am assuming that you have shaped the shoulders with the needles in the holding position, and stripped off with waste yarn — see Chapter Seven 'casting off'). At one time I thought grafting very slow, and I was not always satisfied with the result. But looking at the work of professionals showed me that this could give a perfect finish, and now — after some practice — I can do it quickly and the appearance is very good indeed. (See sketch.) If the

Quick and easy to do and it is used for sewing together almost any type of open edge knitting.

After a little practice you will graft stitches together so well that you cannot afterwards see where your knitwear has been joined.

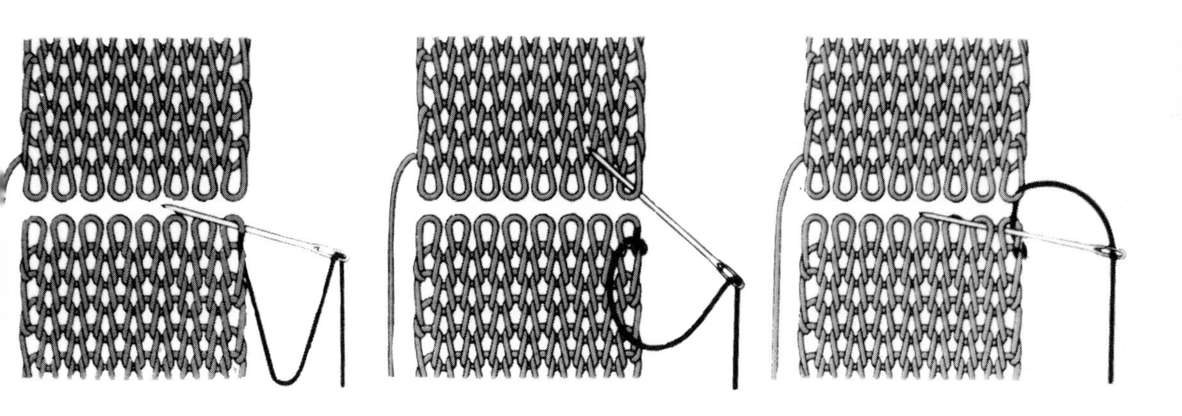

You need a thread of your knitting yarn about 3 times longer than the width of your knitting.

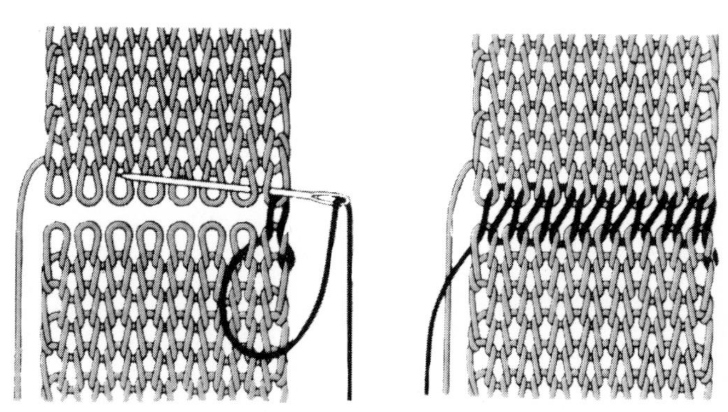

yarn is a very fine, soft one, I find grafting less satisfactory, because although it is still possible to make a good-looking job of it, the fine yarn may stretch on the shoulder. So I then place both lots of stitches back on to the machine, (right sides facing each other), knit one row, cast off either on the machine or with a knitting needle (in this case I strip off with waste yarn). This makes a strong neat shoulder line that does not usually stretch.

If the garment is in fair isle or other stitch pattern (except rib) I cast off, and machine-stitch the shoulders together. This is not only quicker than hand sewing but I think that on the shoulders it gives a much better finish. If the garment is in a rib — or a rib-like stitch — I usually backstitch by hand, making sure that the cast-off edges do not show on the right side.

After joining the shoulders, press the joins carefully — if applicable. Of course, if you have knitted a neckband by picking up the stitches round the neck, you will already have joined one shoulder — to avoid having two joins in the neckband.

Next, complete the neckband (for a sweater). If the band was knitted by picking up stitches with the right side of the work facing you, turn the band to the outside of the garment, and backstitch through the open loops of the last row knitted in main yarn, removing the waste yarn as you go. This needs practice, but it gives a beautiful finish and is well worth spending some time on.

It is important, when finishing a neckband in this way, that the loops into which you will backstitch should be firmly held in some way — you cannot make a good job of the stitching if these loops keep running. With wool (and some synthetics) pressing is all that is necessary. If you are using a synthetic that cannot be pressed (even with a cool iron) then you must find another way; you can damp the last few rows of the neckband and leave them to dry naturally. Or you can run your casting-on cord — or something similar but even finer — through the last row of stitches in main yarn. If the cord is a firm smooth one, there is no danger of your splitting it with your needle — as can happen if you use ordinary knitting yarn.

Always pin the neckband in position, before starting to stitch, and check that your stitching will follow a nice even curve round the neckline. Even neat stitching is useless if the smooth line is marred by 'wiggles' or bumps. Do not begin to stitch until you can see that the neckband will be a good shape when finished.

Any method that achieves a good result is good — and many of you will do as I do: look at top quality professional work, and puzzle out how to achieve the same effect. But to help cautious beginners, here is my method:

After pressing (or damping, or threading the cord through) I unravel all but two rows of the waste yarn. I thread my wool needle with the same yarn as I have used for the garment, and bring it up through the second stitch of the neckband, back and downwards through the first stitch, forward and up through the third stitch, back and down through the second stitch, up through the fourth stitch and so on. Having made a start, I then unravel the waste yarn completely for a few stitches at a time, backstitch through these stitches, unravel waste yarn for a few more stitches — and so on until I have finished the neckband. (See sketch.)

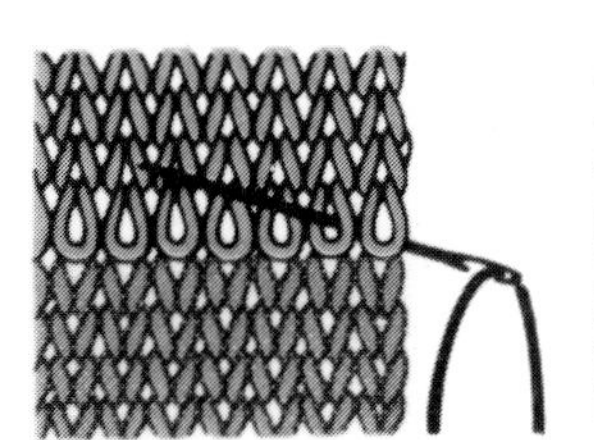

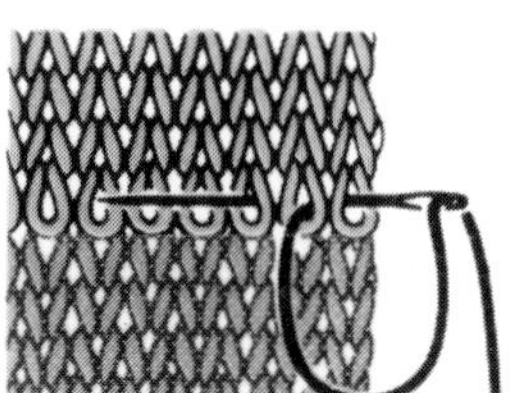

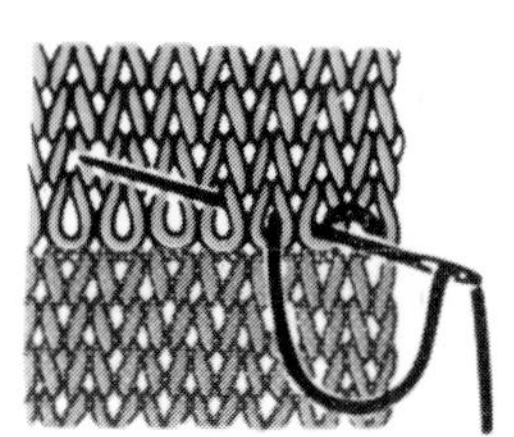

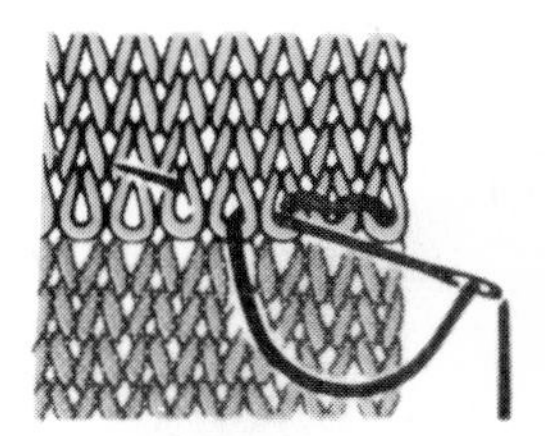

1. Thread tapestry needle with main yarn and, starting at seam edge, bring the needle upwards through second stitch.
2. Insert needle from top into first stitch and through knitting and bring up and through third stitch.
3. Insert from top through second stitch, through knitting and up through fourth stitch.
4. Repeat this backstitch for practice.

I know that some knitters prefer to knit one row with the casting-on cord between the last row knitted in main yarn and the first row knitted in waste yarn. They then sew up with casting-on cord and waste yarn in position, and pull out the casting-on cord (which causes the waste yarn to separate from the main yarn) when the backstitching is finished.

And some knitters always thread a fine cord (or strong sewing thread) through the last row knitted in main yarn — even when they are using pure wool and have been able to press so that the stitches will not run.

When using a casting-on cord *and* pressing, make sure the cord will not be affected by the heat of the iron.

If the band has been knitted by picking up the stitches with the wrong side of the work facing you, turn the band to the inside and slip stitch into position, again removing the waste yarn. If the band has been knitted separately, sew up both shoulders, pin the band into position (take great care with the positioning) stitch through the loops on the right side, then slip stitch the other edge to the inside.

WARNING: if you have picked up your neckband so as to leave holes and gaps — or if you pin on a separately knitted band so that irregularities in the shaping are visible from the right side — then no amount of neat stitching will compensate for this, and give you a good-looking garment. Turn to Chapter Fourteen and try to see where you are going wrong. If necessary, undo the neckband and knit it again. *No garment can look good unless the neckband is good.*

Most of this advice also applies to armhole bands — and if you are making a sleeveless garment, you can either finish your armhole bands as soon as shoulders and neck have been completed, or you can join the side seams first and then complete armhole bands. I prefer the second method, but it is largely a matter of choice.

If the garment is a cardigan or jacket, now is the time to think about front bands.

I am assuming that you are still more or less a beginner — learning fast, but not yet at the stage where you prefer to design your own garments and work out your own patterns. So you should knit the bands just as the pattern tells you — this may be picking up the stitches with the right side of the work facing you (when you will turn the bands to the outside and backstitch through the loops — as described for neckbands) or picking up the stitches with the wrong side of the work facing you (when you will turn the band to the inside and slip stitch into position). Or you may be told to knit the band separately lengthwise — in stocking stitch or a rib — and sew it on. Mattress stitch makes the perfect finish WHEN IT IS WELL DONE, so if you have not yet done so, now is the time to take some small pieces of knitting, study the instructions in your book, and practise until you can do mattress stitch quickly and neatly (you will need it for raglans, too). For the first few cardigans or jackets that you make, follow the pattern instructions absolutely. But a little later you may wish to choose your own method of knitting and attaching bands, so see 'Stitching Bands' in Chapter Seven, and also Chapter Fourteen.

At this stage you may have buttonholes to make. Instructions for these should be given in the book that goes with your machine, but as buttonholes worry many knitters, I am dealing with them more fully in Chapters Fourteen and Sixteen.

We now have to think about Sleeves, and here there is a choice: Many knitters like to put them in before they sew up the sleeve and side seams, so that later they can stitch from cuff to welt in one long seam. They say that not only is this quicker than stitching the seams separately (especially if you do it on the sewing machine) but it is an advantage to be able to open the garment out flat and press the sleeve heads after they have been joined to the armholes.

I use this method if I am dealing with very wide, or square armholes (although I knit these by picking up the stitches round the armholes when I can). But with an ordinary set-in sleeve I have a slight preference for joining side seams, joining sleeve seams, pinning sleeve head into position and then machining.

I think this gives a slightly better appearance. And once again I think that machine stitching is not a substitute for but an improvement on hand-sewing. Even experienced knitters do not always make a good job of hand-sewing in knitted sleeves — I know I never could. I used to avoid these whenever possible, because I always felt they looked slightly home-made. Now that I machine, I achieve a smooth rounded line and a firm appearance that is really satisfactory.

This is the method of making up that I have been using for some years now. It enables me, with very limited spare time, to make garments quickly, with good results. However, it is not the only way to set about making up — other knitters have their own methods, and as I have seen beautiful garments produced by these methods, I should like to mention a few of them:

Some knitters, especially when making up fairly heavy knitwear, like to use a wider zig-zag than I use. Some of them stitch the seam over a fine cord (such as crochet cotton). Several knitters have told me that, with medium or fine yarns, they prefer to make a much wider seam — approximately ½" (1.25 cm) as in dressmaking — and press this open, exactly as if they were using bought material. They add extra stitches, in the knitting, for this seam allowance. Provided the yarn used is not too bulky, and provided it is a material that can be pressed, this can look very good indeed. In fact it is probably much the best way when making up garments that have been woven on the knitting machine. You can use my almost-straight zig-zag, or some knitters simply use a medium-length straight stitch, and of course the elastic straight stitch that the very latest machines do is excellent.

If you want to do a wider seam on a synthetic, that cannot be pressed, you may have to slip stitch the edges of the seam allowance to the main garment — in a mottled, marled or tweedy effect it may be possible to do a row of zig-zag stitching, in a toning sewing thread, down the actual join, working from the right side. Experiment on a small piece of waste knitting.

So far we have been assuming that your garment has set-in sleeves. But of course large numbers of raglan garments are also knitted, and here there is an important difference: raglan sleeves should be joined first (leaving one back shoulder open if you wish to knit the neckband by picking up the stitches round the neck, or replacing the stripped-off stitches on to the machine).

For plain garments, with fully fashioned shaping, mattress stitch gives the best results, and it is worth the trouble for good quality garments. (You can of course machine side and sleeve seams.) With an all-over fair isle, or any other stitch pattern that makes fully fashioned shaping unnecessary (because it will scarcely show) then use either a neat strong back stitch or — if you are pretty competent and can keep a very straight line — machine stitching. You can also 'get away with' machine stitching even on a plain garment if the fully fashioned shapings are several stitches in from the edge, so that they will still be visible after you have joined the pieces together. Keep the seams very straight, press carefully (if applicable) and the result should be quite acceptable. On casual wear or children's play sweaters, some knitters always machine stitch the raglan shapings and then emphasise the join with simple embroidery.

Although we have dealt in detail with only sweaters and jackets, you should now be able to tackle the making up of any knitwear. All making up calls for some dressmaking skill — you should know the basic rules of how to put a garment together. You need not follow these rules slavishly — machine knitting is a very creative hobby, with plenty of

Party dresses for two could be a sizeable item in the family budget. But these little sisters are wearing dream dresses that cost £1.60 for the two. Made on a Knitmaster 323, they are 'the same only different'; the dresses are obviously a pair, apart from the clever way the colours have been alternated.

room for experimenting, innovating and more or less making your own rules. But before you can take hold of the rules and do what you like with them, it is best to know what those rules are.

In Chapter Sixteen I shall be telling you about some of the dressmaking accessories that are really helpful to the machine knitter — and a good *simple* book on dressmaking is one of these 'accessories' (I have suggested several).

I know that a good many knitters start off by saying firmly that they don't like sewing — knitting is their 'thing'. But as you become a better knitter, and produce more and more delightful pieces of knitting, you will be a very unusual person indeed if you do not become keener and keener to gain all the knowledge you can about how to put those beautiful pieces of knitting to the best possible use. *Making up is vital to good knitting.* Most knitters realise that from the beginning. And most of them discover, as they make progress, that it is not only a necessity but an enjoyable, fascinating, absorbing part of the pleasure of machine knitting.

There are other ways of making up that some knitters use with great success:

Crochet:

Pin the two pieces to be joined, with right sides facing. Then simply crochet the pieces together, using an ordinary crochet hook (or the hook supplied with your machine) the main yarn, and double crochet. If the yarn is very thick you may split it, or find a matching, thinner yarn. This does not cover all making-up requirements — such as shoulders, raglans, set-in sleeves etc. But some knitters who are good (and quick) at crochet find it a satisfactory way of dealing with the long seams.

Making Up On The Knitting Machine:

Take the two pieces of knitting and replace the edge stitches on to the machine, right sides of work facing each other. Each needle will have two stitches on it. Knit one row, then cast off according to your instruction book. Some knitters prefer to knit one stitch through the other (by hand) all the way along, and then cast off. This gives a very neat join.

9
The Cut-and-Sew Method

The words 'cut-and-sew' are like a red rag to a bull to some knitters, who say that this method is wasteful and unsatisfactory.

Let us look at these objections.

Is It Wasteful?

Certainly, with this method, you cut off some surplus knitting, which in a sense is 'waste' (though every scrap can be used for stuffing toys or cushions). But dressmakers cut out their garments, and this is not considered wasteful. *And* bought fabrics come in certain standard widths: these are not always economical for the pattern being used, and may result in quite large pieces of 'waste'. With the cut-and-sew method, where you knit or weave your own fabric, you can work to the most economical width and so reduce waste to a minimum. *And* bought materials are much, much more expensive than those we knit or weave ourselves. So it seems to me that the charge of 'wasteful' is unfounded.

Is It Unsatisfactory?

This depends on who is doing the cut-and-sew. I have seen garments where no attempt has been made to finish off well or neaten seams, and of course these garments were unattractive when examined closely (though some of them looked amazingly good in wear). But some dressmakers, using bought fabrics, are just as careless, and the result is the same as with careless cut-and-sew. If knitters, using cut-and-sew methods, take the same trouble as a reasonably good dressmaker takes with her work, then the results can be excellent. And instead of being dependent on finding the material we want — ready made for us — we knitters can produce the design and colour (and width) we want.

I like cut-and-sew. To me, it does not take the place of the traditional shape-as-you-go knitting. But it does widen the scope of wonderful things that can be done with a knitting machine, and enable us to save (and earn) even more, and have even more creative pleasure from our machines.

Before I describe how I use cut-and-sew, there is one important point to make:

It is for YOU to decide how much you will use the cut-and-sew method. I think objections often come from a mistaken idea that once cut-and-sew walks in, there is an end to knitting as we know it. But cut-and-sew is only *one way* of using a knitting machine. It is up to us to use it as much or as little as we please.

I had been machine knitting for nearly ten years before I tried cut-and-sew. I had two things in mind:

(*a*) I wanted to see if I could save time (and trouble) in my own knitting.

(*b*) I wanted to be able to answer the many readers who asked me: "What do you think about cut-and-sew . . ."

I started with a simple garment — a sleeveless top with a U-neck line. It looked like this:

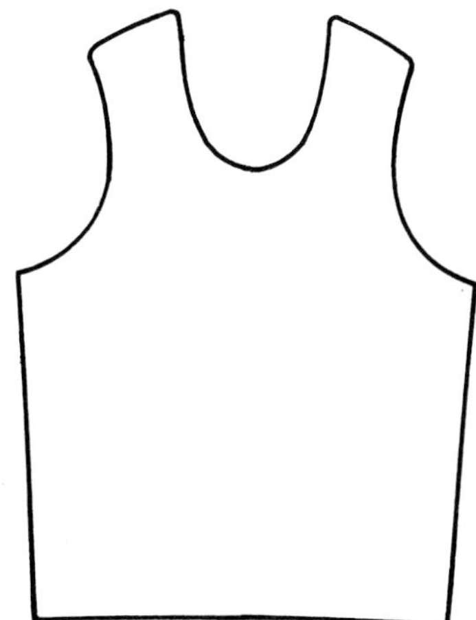

I decided on yarn (a fairly fine coned Shetland), stitch pattern (a small all-over fair isle — I used card No 40 from Knitmaster punch card set M1002) and colours (light and dark blue). I first made this on my Knitmaster 321, later (several times) on the Knitmaster 323. It can be made on any knitting machine, in any suitable stitch pattern, or in plain stocking stitch.

I used a simple dressmaking pattern that I had already made up more than once in bought fabric.

I made a tension square and found that 32 stitches and 44 rows = 4″ (10 cm), which meant 8 stitches and 11 rows to the inch (2.5 cm).

I then looked at the pattern and decided where cut-and-sew would be an advantage.

It would be wasteful — in time and yarn — to knit a piece of fabric wider than the widest part of the garment (which was 18″ - 45 cm). So I cast on 146 stitches (18 × 8 = 144, plus one extra stitch each side for the seam allowance = 146). The side seam measured 14″ (35 cm) (including hem) so I knitted 154 rows (14 × 11 = 154). This brought me to the armholes.

Now it would have been very easy to work out the armhole shaping. I could see that from 18″ (45 cm) I had to decrease to 12″ (30 cm) which would mean reducing the 146 stitches to 96 stitches (I should not need the extra stitch each side, for seam allowance, since the armholes would be bound with braid). Many knitters find this so easy to do that they do not think it worth while to use cut-and-sew at this point — and usually I agree with them, but on this occasion I wanted to try out the method, so I decided to continue knitting straight to the highest point — 23″ (57.5 cm). I knitted until the row counter read 254 rows (11 × 23 = 253 but I always like to work with even numbers).

I knitted front and back the same — though I could have knitted one continuous strip, long enough for front and back plus shoulder seam allowance. I then washed and pressed the pieces (the washing was necessary only because I was using an oiled Shetland wool). I laid the paper pattern on the back, and carefully pinned round the outline of armholes, shoulders and neck (some knitters prefer to mark with chalk, or to tack). I did the same with the front of the garment.

Using a suitable thread (see Chapter Eight) in a contrasting colour I straight stitched (medium length) round the outlines I had marked, removing the pins as I went. I chose a contrasting colour because the stitching would not be seen, when the garment was completed, and the contrast made it easier for me to see where I had to cut. For stitching that will show I naturally use a matching thread, or if this is impossible then one of the translucent threads.

I did another row of straight stitching, about ⅛″ (3 mm) inside the first (I often omit this now, but this was my first cautious attempt). I then did a row of zig-zag stitching — medium width, medium length — positioning it so that the needle pierced the fabric very close to the cutting line, but never outside it.

I gave the pieces another light pressing. Then I cut out exactly as if I were using bought fabric but being very careful not to cut the machine stitching. The stitching itself held the loose threads in place: there seemed to be no tendency to fray — and since I was using wool and had pressed with a fairly hot iron and a damp cloth, I believe I could have omitted the stitching without disaster. But I still — almost always — stitch before cutting. It takes only a few minutes, and is a good safeguard.

I then machined up the shoulders, using matching thread, and pressed the seam open. The edges were neat, the join was firm and straight, but as the fair isle design had produced rather a thick fabric, I thought the double thickness made by folding back the seam allowance was rather clumsy, and decided it would have been better to shape the shoulders in the usual way. I almost always do this, now. (But in a jacket or other outer garment, the thickness could be quite acceptable.)

Next I machined the side seams. As these were joined only one stitch in, there was no seam allowance to produce bulk.

This left neck and armholes to finish. The dressmaking pattern gave instructions for binding with braid, so I followed the pattern exactly, using a bought braid that matched the dark blue. I could also have knitted a plain braid, in either of the two colours, or I could have knitted neck band and armhole bands and attached them in the usual way. It would have been a simple matter of calculating the number of stitches to cast on and the number of rows to knit.

I turned up the hem (following the pattern instructions) and slip stitched it into place. I could also have used hemming web — I often do, now.

I found this garment quick and easy to do, and it looked very good indeed. It was the simplest possible exercise in cut-and-sew, but it taught me a great deal.

Since then I have used cut-and-sew on many occasions, but usually to a limited extent. I shape wherever I can easily do so (and this usually includes armhole and shoulder shaping), cut-and-sew where this saves time and trouble (for necklines and awkward shapes).

I am sure that if knitters who have so far fought shy of this method would do as I did — start with something very simple and take an objective look at the advantages of cut-and-sew — they would lose their distrust of it and find it a very useful addition to their knitting skill.

Of course, some professional knitters use cut-and-sew in a different way. They are tolerantly amused at my cautious approach. But this book is for the amateur who — however expert she may become — is still working under home conditions.

The professional knitter who uses cut-and-sew simply knits or weaves fabric, usually in one continuous length and sometimes not even working out the most economical width, and uses it exactly as bought fabric. And this produces wonderful results and is very fast. BUT it calls for more dressmaking skills than some of us possess (my way needs only elementary knowledge). And these professional knitters are often part of a team — one knits or weaves, another presses and marks out, another stitches and cuts, another makes up . . . Those of us who knit at home usually have to do everything ourselves. We cannot always duplicate workroom conditions and so we have to work out our own methods. And in my opinion it is often easier, pleasanter and just as quick to shape wherever we can and save cut-and-sew for only a few operations.

But it is experience that teaches. Once you have done a few very simple cut-and-sew garments you will gain confidence and want to experiment and branch out. You may find you are using it more and more — almost to the exclusion of shaping as you go. You may find you prefer to do as I do. There is no right and wrong way for this: if it works (which means that it saves you time and produces attractive garments), it is right.

I have done a good deal of experimenting with cut-and-sew: some of the things I have learned are:

(*1*) Even long seams — such as the side seams of a jacket or skirt — do not seem to fray if pressed (where possible) and stitched as I have already described. I prefer to knit to width (shaping skirt panels if necessary) but I have tried out the other way. Knitters with scissors fright should try this out for themselves, using oddments of yarn.

(*2*) When using wool, you can open the seams and press them back, just as with bought fabric.

(*3*) With synthetic yarns (occasionally with a mixture of wool and synthetic) pressing may not be possible. I have sometimes pressed such seams open with my fingers and lightly slip stitched the edges back on to the garment. I have also worked a row of zig-zag stitching along the seam line, working from the right side. If you are using a marled, random or tweed wool, and can find a thread that matches one of the colours, this scarcely shows. Even on a plain fabric, a matching thread, worked neatly, looks quite good. Of course, some synthetics can be pressed, and then the problem does not arise.

(All the above remarks refer to true cut-and-sew — when the material has been cut the whole length of the fabric and then stitched up. When the straight parts of a garment are knitted to width, with just one stitch allowed for the seams — as described before — there is no problem. This is the way I prefer.)

(*4*) If I cut-and-sew sleeve heads, I like to finish off by binding with tape or bias binding (after the sleeve has been put into the armhole).

(*5*) I make full use of all the dressmaking aids that help me when I am sewing with bought materials (see Chapter Sixteen).
(*6*) You can if you wish start off the back and front, or the sleeve, of a cut-and-sew garment with the appropriate knitted welt or cuff.
(*7*) You can if you wish do a cut-and-sew neckline and still pick up the stitches for the neckband — be sure to pick up very evenly, well inside the stitching.
(*8*) With a deep U or V shaped neckline, or a wide boat-shape, you can reinforce the edge, if you wish, with tape or bias binding. Or by working a row of zig-zag stitching over a fine cord (such as crochet cotton).
(*9*) My own cut-and-sew is done with the same sewing machine as my other making up (see Chapter Eight). If you do not have a swing-needle machine, then do two rows of straight stitching, and check very carefully that all knitted stitches are firmly held and cannot fray or run. If any stitches seem to have been missed, catch them in by hand.
(*10*) Use sharp scissors and cut smoothly — avoid a line of little jagged notches, and be careful not to cut into the zig-zag stitching.
(*11*) If, on a high round neckline without an opening, you feel that the straight stitching will make the neck too tight, omit this and use just the row of zig-zag stitching. (Some modern sewing machines have an elastic straight stitch, which is very good.)
(*12*) Avoid fair isle patterns with long floats — unless you are going to line your garment or back it with iron-on interfacing. Even if you line it — by which I mean make a separate lining and stitch it inside the garment, you may find yourself in some difficulty. If you mount your knitting — which means backing it with fabric and then cutting out and sewing the two fabrics as if they were only one, the difficulties will be less, but this calls for a good knowledge of fabrics, because top fabric and mounting must have the same washing and wearing qualities and the same amount of stretch.
(*13*) Handle lace and punch card lace with great care. This does not mean that it cannot be used for cut-and-sew (Knitmaster recently showed me a wedding dress, made with lengths of knitted punch card lace, from a Vogue pattern, and it was beautiful). But they do need care (so do bought lace fabrics).
(*14*) Explore the possibilities of slip stitch patterns in fine yarns — they can give very firm, attractive fabrics.
(*15*) Remember that weaving (which can be done on many modern machines) is ideal for cut-and-sew. Too many knitters ignore their machine's ability to weave.
(*16*) When working from a dressmaking pattern, you must knit in the direction of the straight-of-grain mark. You must also position the

pattern, on your knitted or woven fabric, just as carefully as if you were using shop-bought material.

(*17*) Not all fabrics are suitable for all purposes. It is tempting to try off-beat experiments, but you cannot expect to use a fine lacy fabric for a tailored garment and get the same effect as you would with a gaberdine or denim.

So far we have talked about 'your pattern' without making it clear where you get your pattern.

You can use:

Simple Dressmaking Patterns

Avoid lots of fussy detail, gussets etc and keep darts to a minimum. Most commercial pattern books have a VERY EASY section, and usually a section of patterns especially designed for knitted fabrics.

Diagram Patterns

Many magazines publish these from time to time (e.g. *Home Sewing and Knitting, Pins and Needles, Living* etc). I find these good to work from — they are simple, well fitting and attractive. Remember when you are cutting out patterns from diagrams — to use with cut-and-sew — you need make a pattern only of the shaped pieces. If the back of a garment consists of one straight piece of knitting, from hem to armhole, there is no need to make a paper pattern of that section, because it is so very simple to work out the number of stitches to cast on and the number of rows to knit (look back to my description of my own first attempt at cut-and-sew, in this chapter).

Diagrams In Machine Knitting Pattern Books

These are ideal, because they will be eminently suitable for machine knitting.

Simple, Well Fitting Garments

that you already own will make good patterns.

And of course you can work from PRINTED KNITTING PATTERNS, by obtaining the right tension, following the pattern for all the straight-forward parts, and then using cut-and-sew for the 'tricky' bits. Very often this is only the neckline, and simply means that you shape armholes and shoulders and then strip off with waste yarn — for back and front alike. Even this limited use of cut-and-sew is a tremendous time-saver.

In addition to saving time, cut-and-sew means that necklines etc can be adjusted after the garment has been tacked and tried on. This is sometimes particularly important with the back neckline. Most garments fit better if the back neckline is slightly shaped (it does away with the roll that spoils some knitwear). But this slows down knitting quite a bit, and a lot of knitters decide not to bother (and then may be disappointed when the garment is finished). Cut-and-sew is a quick way of shaping the back neckline, and can greatly improve your knitwear.

Cut-and-sew also means that you can knit items for which no suitable knitting pattern may be available. Things are improving, but up to the moment there are not — in my view — enough patterns for things like capes, ponchos, shaped stoles, caftans, housecoats, leisure gowns, cap-sleeved shrugs and other casual garments that are expensive to buy but very attractive to wear. Cut-and-sew is also a great help with home furnishing — for covering odd shaped cushions, chairs etc. As long as you have the old cover as a pattern, you can knit or weave the material and save a good deal of money, as well as making an excellent job of it.

And of course it has a definite place in make-do-and-mend. It can be much quicker and easier to knit or weave a small piece of fabric and cut out the new yoke, or collar, or whatever you need, than to work out a knitting pattern and knit to shape.

Perhaps most important of all, cut-and-sew enables knitters — especially if they are inexperienced, or rather timid, or have very little time for their knitting, or work under difficult conditions — to tackle (successfully) knitting that otherwise might have been put off indefinitely.

I think there is no doubt that necklines spell disaster for many knitters. They quickly learn how to shape them in stocking stitch, but when it comes to stitch patterns, the thought of the dividing and shaping makes their hearts sink — and back they go to the old classic stocking stitch.

So far, no machine can do real Aran knitting. But by clever use of hand cabling (which does not slow the knitting down too much) and separately knitted, and sewn on, cords, plaits and bobbles, attractive Aran-type garments can be produced. This is a garment designed and knitted up by a fairly new knitter.

This is quite understandable. If you are working in a stitch pattern, on an older machine, neck shaping can be very tricky indeed, and it is easy to make a mistake. On a double bed machine you may have to cope with pushers and a racking handle, as well as remembering to keep the shaping correct. Even with a modern punch card machine — which makes patterning really easy — shaping a neckline needs a certain amount of skill and experience — *much less* than with simpler machines, but still some. You have to note the number of the pattern panel and row counter, and when you have finished one side of the neck you must reset the machine correctly so that you get the right row in the stitch pattern . . . I know this is very easy, with a good modern machine, but it is not foolproof, and most of the mistakes that infuriate knitters are made while shaping necklines.

Professional knitters cannot always understand this. I have seen the look of pitying astonishment on their faces when I have mentioned it. But they work under ideal conditions: the amateur knitter — even if she is trying to earn a living with her machine — often works in unavoidable difficulties. The telephone rings, a child rushes in with a cut knee, the cat wants to be let out, the pinger announces that the pie should come out of the oven . . . This is when mistakes happen, and this is why I like cut-and-sew necklines.

10
Saving with your Knitting Machine

Saving is built into your knitting machine.

It is one of the main purposes of machine knitting, and to some extent the whole of this book is one long lesson on saving. So this chapter is by no means complete in itself — it simply gathers up a few economy ideas that have not appeared under other headings.

Combining Knitting and Sewing

is one of the cleverest ways of saving — it enables you to take advantage of bargains in both yarns and fabrics, and to make use of left-overs. Sometimes small amounts of really beautiful fabrics are sold very cheaply, but the snag is the difficulty of finding matching or toning fabric to go with them. This is much easier with a knitting machine, which enables you to make your own fabric.

Saving On Luxury

sounds contradictory — but even when money is tight, most of us need at least one 'party' outfit, and this can be a worrying expense if we have to buy ready-made, or even buy fabric and make our own. Machine knitted evening wear can be really cheap and look really good — knitted lace, lurex type yarn, some of the shiny rayons, woven fabric with the look of rich brocade can all make evening wear that looks elegant and is warm without being grannified. A knitted stole or cape makes a super evening cover-up (often more expensive than the dress). And often — depending on the yarn — you can unravel your evening dress, when you are tired of it, and knit it up into something quite different.

Dressmakers will point out that making your own clothes — with the sewing machine and bought fabric — has all these advantages, and this is almost true. But knitted fabrics have special advantages. And when you buy a fabric, you can be reasonably sure that hundreds of other women, living within reach of the store where you shopped, will also have bought it . . . When you machine knit your clothes, using your own combination of yarn(s), stitch patterns, designs and colours, you can make yourself an original model — and only excessively unlucky coincidence could make you shout 'snap' at another guest.

Machine Knitting is Ideal for Renovations

Dresses and jackets with shabby sleeves can be renovated by knitting new sleeves and sewing these in with the sewing machine — exactly as if they were made of bought material. But while sleeves of a different ready-made material tend to look 'conjured up', knitted sleeves — especially if you add a knitted collar, tie belt etc — often improve the appearance of a garment.

To knit the sleeves you can use any of these methods:

(*a*) Measure the depth of the armholes on the dress, and the width across top of sleeve (before the cap shaping starts), look through your knitting patterns and see whether you have a knitted sleeve pattern that will fit without alteration. Since armholes and sleeves are largely standard, you stand quite a good chance of doing so.

(*b*) You may not find a pattern which fits exactly, but you may easily find one that fits with only a slight alteration — say 1″ (2.5 cm) more or less on the height of the sleeve head. It is easy to make this small alteration.

Say you are knitting at a tension of 10 rows = 1″ (2.5 cm), then you will need to knit ten rows more, or less, than given in the pattern.

If you study sleeve patterns, you will find that the height of the sleeve head is usually about two-thirds of the depth of the armhole, and that the shaping of the sleeve head starts by decreasing a block of stitches — approx. 4 to approx. 7 is fairly common. This may be followed by a number of smaller decreases. (Let us call these two operations Step 1 and Step 2.) Knit these two steps according to the pattern.

Next we come to Step 3, and quite often this involves decreasing one stitch at each end of every alternate row. I like to add length at this point — so if I want to make the sleeve head taller than the pattern, I work the extra rows into this section. This means that if I have to work an extra ten rows, I shall have to make the first ten decreases every *third* row instead of every second row. I shall have knitted ten extra rows, but arrived at the same number of stitches.

Since this is a process you may often wish to use — with different numbers of stitches, different intervals of decreasing etc — let us go through an example in detail. I have opened the first machine knitting pattern book on my shelf and taken the first pattern with set-in sleeves.

It is a child's pattern — the number of stitches before starting to shape the sleeve head is 86; there are 11 rows to the inch, and as I want to make the sleeve head 1″ (2.5 cm) taller, I shall have to work 11 extra rows in to the shaping.

The pattern says:

Step 1 "Cast off 4 stitches at the beginning of the next 2 rows (this will leave 78 stitches and the row counter will read 2)

Step 2 Cast off 2 stitches at the beginning of the next 2 rows (this will leave 74 stitches and the row counter will read 4)

Step 3 Decrease 1 stitch at each end of every alternate row 14 times . . . (46 stitches will remain, and the row counter will read 32)

Now we will make the alteration — adding the extra 11 rows.

Steps 1 and *2* will be the same.

Step 3: we need to 'smuggle in' the extra eleven rows, so we will add one row, eleven times. This means decreasing (for the first eleven decreases) every third row instead of every second row, after which we can work the remaining three decreases every alternate row, as the pattern says. To make it easier, put the row counter back to 0. Decrease when the row counter reads 3, 6, 9, 12, 15, 18, 21, 24, 27, 30, 33 (11 decreases). Now decrease the remaining three times every second row — when the row counter reads 35, 37, 39.

We have already worked 4 rows on steps 1 and 2 — add these to the row counter reading of 39 and we have 43, which is eleven more rows than we had when we followed the pattern exactly, and this is what we need to give us the extra inch in height.

I have gone through this very simple alteration step by step because once you start to alter patterns to your individual requirements (and you will want to do this, very soon) you may often need to make this type of alteration. Perhaps you will need to lengthen or shorten a pattern — if it is a straight piece of knitting, you calculate the number of rows more or less that you will need and simply add or subtract them. But if the piece of knitting is shaped, you cannot do this — you must work them in smoothly so that the shaping is only slightly altered. You can see the necessity for this if you imagine what would have happened if you had added the eleven extra rows, all in one straight piece, to the sleeve head. Whether you added them after step 1 or after step 2 or at the top of the sleeve head, you would have finished up with a very odd shape.

The actual figures I have quoted — taken from a pattern chosen at random — may be no good to you at all (it is unlikely that you will want to make such a large alteration on such a small pattern). But I wanted to show you the *principle* of working in extra rows, because you may need it many times, not only on sleeve heads but on the shaped section of a sleeve, skirt panels etc etc.

If I want to make the sleeve head shorter than the pattern, I do it very easily by simply omitting the last ten rows. This makes a flatter, less shaped sleeve head; I have done it many times, over a good many years of knitting, and I have always been pleased with the result. I know other knitters who prefer to knit according to the pattern, strip off the last block of stitches, run a thread through the last row of knitting, and ease the top in slightly to fit the armhole.

Whichever way you adopt, you should measure the armhole of the dress after you have removed the old sleeves. If for any reason you have to cut away any material — say it is too tight, or it has become worn or frayed — this must be taken into account when knitting the new sleeves. Remember to allow seam allowance, too.

(*c*) Reasonably skilled dressmakers sometimes prefer to use a knitted sleeve pattern that they know fits them well, and adjust the armhole of the dress to fit this.

(*d*) You can weave, or knit, your fabric and make sleeves by the cut-and-sew method (see Chapter Nine). In this case, use the old sleeve as a pattern.

(*e*) If you have a Knit Radar or Knit Leader, you can make a pattern block from the old sleeve and knit to size and shape, in any stitch pattern or yarn of your choice (see Chapter Twelve).

(*f*) Using a simple dressmaking pattern, you can alter the armhole to square, deep or dolman. This usually avoids a shaped sleeve head (or substitutes one that is only very slightly shaped); it is quick and easy and can look very good (try out the effect by pinning in a mock sleeve of any odd material).

Another way of dealing with a dress with shabby sleeves is to turn it into a pinafore dress by removing sleeves, scooping out armholes and neckline, and finishing with braid. Braid is expensive, and you cannot always find the colour you want, but you can knit it (cheaply) on your machine — and this has the following advantages:

You can use the same wool to knit a belt — with other accessories such as hat, bag etc.

You can knit a matching sweater which will give you, in effect, a dress again, but with new sleeves and neckline, and double warmth.

You can knit striped or fair isle sweaters, using the same wool as the braid, with one or more contrasting colours.

If you have knitted your braid in a fine yarn, you can use one strand of this with one (or more) of another colour and get a mottled, random or tweedy effect, where one of the colours exactly matches the braid.

You can wear the pinafore dress with a plain white shirt or sweater and make a jacket in the same wool as the braid.

If you look at clothes in some of the better stores, you will see that it is this perfect matching — often in non-standard colours — that gives many outfits their expensive look. It can be achieved — cheaply — on your knitting machine.

Braid

---

can be knitted with even the simplest knitting machine — it need be no more than a strip of plain stocking stitch, which can be used with either the knit or the purl side as the right side. If you want to make a fold line, leave one needle out of working position. If you prefer a narrow braid, that will have a rounded appearance, leave all needles in working position. Even if you do not normally make up your knitwear on the sewing machine, you should not find it difficult to machine this kind of braid into position — sew with the right sides of the work facing, then turn the braid to the inside and slip stitch into position.

Semi-automatic machines can knit braids in simple tuck stitch patterns (you should have instructions; if not, experiment with various stitches). If you have a double bed machine or a ribbing attachment with a racking device, a close rib, racked alternately to right and left every two rows, is effective. So is fisherman's rib, treated in the same way. (NOTE: some instruction books use the word 'rack', some 'swing'; some refer to 'fisherman's rib', some to 'English rib'). Double bed machines (or ribbing attachments) can also make good braid by doing two rows of close ribbing, two rows of tubular knitting, alternately. Or by using 'longstitch' which is one bed set for tubular knitting, one bed set for normal knitting. I often use an ordinary every-needle rib, with four stitches on the back bed, two stitches on the front bed. Some of these braids have to be stitched, flat, to the knitting; they are not all suitable for binding the edges.

The more sophisticated machines make use of some beautiful braids in some of their patterns — follow instructions for your particular machine. And machines that do automatic two-colour work can make braids in tiny all-over fair isle — tweed stitch or tiny checks or vertical or diagonal stripes — look through your punch cards for interesting ideas.

These simple fair isle patterns can also be done on simple machines. As you will be knitting a long length, it would be rather slow — but the effect could be excellent.

There are many more ways to rescue a dress that — without such help — would be on its way to the jumble sale. And renovations apply to coats, skirts, jackets, housecoats — in fact all kinds of garments, as well

It's young, trendy, and could have stepped right out of the pages of a glossy magazine. But in fact it was designed and made by a knitter who was just completing her postal tuition course and not by a professional designer.

as dresses. Many magazines feature renovations, and some of the commercial dressmaking patterns make use of two different fabrics for the same garment, which usually means you can adapt the idea for a renovation. There is no point in my repeating, here, what you can read and see in so many other places, so all I want to do is make you realise what a wonderful ally your knitting machine is, in the game of make-do-and-mend. It means you can actually produce that piece of fabric that otherwise you might spend days hunting and then have to pay quite a lot for. Your machine will knit it quickly, easily and *cheaply*. And if you still feel it might be difficult to work out a pattern for the sleeves, collar, yoke or whatever else you need to update a garment, then cut-and-sew is the answer (see Chapter Nine).

Machine knitters can make great savings in home furnishings too — I have mentioned this in previous chapters. Good furnishing fabrics are expensive, knitted or woven ones are *very much* cheaper — especially as some of the cheap coned synthetics make good background yarns for weaving.

You cannot, unfortunately in some ways, produce materials as wide as those you can buy. But — as with cut-and-sew — you can often save still further by working out the most economical width for your requirements and working to that (or a fraction of that, if you have to join). Where a join is essential, as it will be for really big items such as bed spreads, it can be done unobtrusively with a sewing machine (and remember, you will probably have to join even bought materials for a bed spread) or you can make a feature of the joins with contrasting braid or knitted inserts.

For maximum saving, you should learn something about yarns — so that you will know which are suitable for your knitting machine (see Chapter Thirteen). With this basic knowledge, you should be able to take advantage of bargain lots, wool sales, markets — and other sources of cheap yarns. Don't rush in, and buy a lot of cheap yarn, until you have had a little experience of what yarns knit up well. And NEVER buy harsh, hairy yarns. They will not make up into nice garments, and they could damage your machine. This is NOT saving.

You should also send for shade cards to all the leading mail order firms and if possible you should decide on one — or two — regular suppliers and then talk to him (them) about a discount for quantity. You might get together with other knitters in your area, order in really substantial quantities, and so earn yourselves quite an interesting concession. In any case, with postage so expensive, it will pay you to order in large lots, and not in frequent small quantities. (Many of the mail order firms send post free above a certain amount.)

11
Tension — the Basis of Good Knitting

Sometimes knitters go along very happily, using printed patterns and the recommended yarns, and producing excellent garments. And then (rightly) they decide to branch out — to alter patterns to individual requirements, to design their own simple garments, to use different yarns and stitch patterns. And — in some cases — suddenly nothing goes right any longer.

The reason for this setback is almost always that they have not grasped the fact that *to knit to size, you must get your tension right.*

If you have a modern knitting machine, your instruction book almost certainly gives you a good, easy way to make a tension square. With older machines, you may be told to knit a small test piece and measure the number of stitches and rows to the inch.

This is not very satisfactory; there are far better ways of measuring tension.

In the first place, measuring the rows and stitches to one square inch is not sufficient. It is very easy to make a mistake, when measuring, and one tiny mistake every inch can become a large mistake when it goes right across a full-size garment. So the first rule is to work over a larger area — *at least* 4" square (10 cm), preferably more.

In the second place, actually measuring stitches and rows is a tricky thing to do (can be a nightmare for anyone whose eyesight is not good for close work) and becomes difficult and confusing when you are working in — say — a tuck stitch where some stitches do not knit on every row.

So the obvious thing is to work out how much a certain number of stitches and rows should measure, and then aim at producing those measurements.

Let's start with a very easy example. Suppose you want to knit a pattern where 26 stitches and 34 rows = 4" (10 cm). This is the way you will probably see the tension given in the pattern, but if you are using a pattern that still works to the square inch, you will see 6½ stitches and

8½ rows = 1″ (2.5 cm) — so you simply multiply by four, which gives you 26 stitches and 34 rows.

If the pattern has been written especially for your machine, there may be a stitch size given — in this instance it could be around 7. But remember *this is for guidance only*. Knitting machines — although the good ones are such wonderful pieces of engineering — vary a little (where I use a stitch size 7, another knitter with the same machine may need 6.. or even 6., or 7.). And two different knitters, taking it in turns to use the same machine, can also get slightly different tensions — one may press down harder on the cam box than the other, one may tend to push the cam box towards the back, another towards the front . . . there are all sorts of things which can make a tiny variation in the size of the stitches, and the depth of the rows. When you see a tension given, with a stitch size beside it, remember this is a starting point from which you can experiment — it is not an order that you have to follow blindly.

But it may be that the pattern you are using was written for another make of machine; if you study machine knitting patterns you will soon get to know which other machines have stitch sizes that roughly correspond to those on your machine. So, again, the stitch size given in the pattern may be a good starting point for you.

Or you may be using a pattern that is written for any machine — in this case no stitch size will be given. This terrifies beginners, but is not as frightening as it looks. Before you start on a garment, you should have done lots of practice pieces — and probably lots of scarves or cushion covers or other simple shapes (see Chapter Six), so you will have a general idea of what stitch size is suitable for the different types of yarn — in other words, you will know the *approximate* stitch size, which is all you will know even if the pattern gives a figure.

Take a ball of wool as near the thickness of the main yarn as possible, but a different colour. Start with a stitch size one point smaller than the one mentioned in the pattern, or the one you have estimated. By 'one point' I do not mean one whole stitch size — i.e. NOT stitch size 6 if the pattern states stitch size 7, but stitch size 6.. (6 and two dots on the stitch size dial). This is the marking on my Knitmaster 323 and on some other machines. However, you may have a machine where the sizes are differently marked and divided. For instance, on the Passap Duomatic you will see stitch sizes 1 to 8, with a half-way mark between the numbers. Although not numbered on the dial, there are ¼ and ¾ settings too — just one click of the dial. Whichever way the stitch sizes are numbered, and however they are divided, the principle is the same: when you are testing out various stitch sizes to get the right number of rows and stitches, start as small as you reasonably can, and work up one stage at a time.

Cast on about 60 stitches and knit not less than 1″ (2.5 cm). Break off the contrast wool and start to knit with the yarn you are going to knit the garment in (this is usually called 'the main yarn').

Knit 17 rows with main yarn (17 = half 34). Then push forward the 14th needle to the right and to the left of the centre needle (which means that there are 26 needles in between the two you have pushed forward). With a short piece of contrast yarn knit by hand the two needles you have pushed forward (this is only to mark them, so that you will know where to measure). Knit another 17 rows with main yarn, change to contrast yarn, knit a few rows, change back to main yarn, but with your stitch size one point higher (that is, it will now be at the size which the pattern gave or which you guessed). Do the same as you did before — knit 17 rows, mark the 14th needle to left and right of centre, knit another 17 rows, change to contrast — then repeat in main yarn but with a stitch size one point higher. Finally knit at least 1″ (2.5 cm) rows with waste yarn and strip off.

Take hold of the waste yarn at top and bottom of your knitting and give the knitting a firm lengthwise pull. Don't tug or jerk — just pull for a moment. Then leave the knitting alone for at least two hours. Next, treat it exactly as you would treat a garment knitted in the yarn — if it is an oiled Shetland, then you must wash it etc (see Chapter Thirteen). If it is non-oiled wool, you will press the garment with a fairly hot iron and damp cloth — so do the same with the tension square (but not if it is rib or raised stitch). If it is a synthetic, you may not be able to press at all — or only very lightly with a cool iron and dry cloth, so treat your tension square in the same way.

When the tension square is dry and cold, measure the size of the knitting between the two needles marked with contrast yarn, and between the rows knitted in contrast. One of these squares should give you the correct measurement — 4″ (10 cm) square.

If none of the pieces of knitting measures 4″ (10 cm), then look at the texture of the knitting. Let's assume that the nearest to the right measurement is the largest stitch size you have tried, but this is still too small. If that piece of knitting is already on the loose side, there is no point in trying a larger stitch size, because even if you achieve the right measurements, you will not have a nice firm fabric that will make a satisfactory garment.

This is where novice knitters sometimes despair and feel they will never get the hang of machine knitting. But things are not hopeless!

I assume — in this imaginary problem — that you have *not* used the yarn recommended in the pattern. If you have, then you should be able to achieve the given tension. And ideally — there is no doubt about this — you *should* use the yarn recommended in the pattern. Publishers of knitting patterns (hand and machine) constantly warn us that unless we use the yarn they specify they cannot guarantee good results — and this is a perfectly fair warning, because the pattern was designed for one particular yarn. But years of experience with machine knitting and machine knitters have taught me that this is a rule all of us break, pretty often. We know that if the pattern says X's 'Easiknit', then we ought to go down to the shops and buy X's 'Easiknit'. But we may not have time to go to the shops; our local shops may not stock it; it may be too expensive, or not made in the colour we want; if it is a mail order yarn we may be in too much of a hurry to wait; we may have been asked to knit up some other yarn; we may have bought a bargain in a sale and want to use it up . . . in short, there are a lot of reasons why, though we know we ought to use the recommended yarn, we quite often do not do so. In addition to this, yarns come and go — like everything else — and we may find a pattern that is exactly what we want, but the recommended yarn is no longer made. Or we may be working from a Continental or American pattern, and the exact wool may not be obtainable.

So we are left with our tension squares, and none of these comes up to the right measurement.

If the appearance and 'feel' of the knitted fabric show that you could use a stitch size smaller or larger, and still have a nice fabric, then go on experimenting until either you have the right measurement, or you get to the point where the fabric will be too loose and open, or too tight and hard, to be satisfactory.

Sometimes you may find that you can produce a nice fabric where the given number of stitches measures 4" (10 cm) across, but the given number of rows is a little too long or too short. You can try altering the setting of the yarn brake/tension spring. This may make just enough difference to give you the correct measurement. If the yarn runs more freely, then the knitting will be a fraction looser (which means your piece of knitting will be slightly longer); if the yarn is 'braked' a little, then the knitting will be a fraction tighter, and your tension square will be just a little shorter. Sometimes this solves the problem.

Sometimes, when you cannot achieve the right measurements, you can 'change' the yarn by adding another strand. For instance, if you are using a coned synthetic, possibly working with three strands, then you could try four strands (if your tension square is too small) or two strands (if your tension square is too large). Sometimes, with Shetland wool, you can add a very fine 1-ply Shetland (this yarn is too fine to knit on its own, but sometimes comes in handy for using with thicker Shetlands), or a

Very often it is the accessories — the hat and scarf to go with the sweater or jacket — that make it so expensive to be well dressed. With a knitting machine, fashion extras can be made quickly and cheaply. Hat and scarf shown here are knitted in fisherman's rib, on a double bed machine. But attractive accessories can be made on any machine.

fine lambswool. Unless you have the exact colour, this will change the appearance as well as the thickness of the yarn, but as Shetland colours tend to be misty or mottled, this is not necessarily a disadvantage — in fact some very attractive effects can result from this thickening up. (See Chapter Thirteen for more information about yarns.)

If you still fail to get the right measurements — after trying all this — then abandon the idea of using that particular yarn with that particular pattern. There are various ways of getting round this (see Chapter Twelve) but for the moment I want to concentrate on showing you that if the tension square says NO, then you should accept that.

Suppose you decide to risk it. You think it's near enough . . . What happens?

Your tension square measures 3¾″ × 4¼″ (9.375 × 10.625 cm), when it should have measured 4″ × 4″ (10 × 10 cm) — but you decide to go ahead and knit the sweater. You want your garment to measure 40″ (100 cm) round the chest and 28″ (70 cm) long. This is what it would measure if your tension square measured 4″ × 4″ (10 × 10 cm).

So you follow the pattern and cast on 130 stitches and (we are disregarding shaping for the moment) you knit 238 rows (28 × 8½).

Now in every 26 stitches you lose ¼″ (.625 cm) (because your tension piece measured only 3¾″ (9.375 cm) when it ought to have measured 4″ (10 cm)). There are ten blocks of 26 stitches round front and back of the sweater (2 × 130 = 260 stitches) so you lose 10 × ¼″ = 2½″ (6.25 cm). Your sweater will measure 37½ inches (93.75 cm) instead of 40″ (100 cm) — it won't fit.

Let's complete the exercise by looking at the length. In every 34 rows you will have ¼″ (0.625 cm) more than you should have, because your tension square measured 4¼″ (10.625 cm) instead of 4″ (10 cm). And there are seven lots of 34 rows, so you will have 7 × ¼″ more than you should have = 1¾″ (4.375 cm), so it will measure 29¾″ (74.375 cm) instead of the 28″ (70 cm) you wanted — and again, IT WON'T FIT.

I have gone into this at great length — experienced knitters may feel it is boring length — because until novice knitters realise the absolute necessity of working to tension they cannot produce garments that come up to the right size, and therefore cannot be really successful knitters.

One more important point to remember (beginners sometimes overlook this) is that if you are going to knit a garment in more than one stitch pattern, you must do a tension square for each stitch pattern. There may be quite a difference in both stitches and rows. And if you do a number of garments in fair isle, using the same yarn but different fair isle designs, then you may have to do a tension square for each design.

We all know that fair isle sometimes pulls the work in, making a fair isle tension square smaller than a stocking stitch tension square knitted with the same yarn, on the same stitch size (or even one size larger for the fair isle, as most patterns recommend). But some fair isle designs pull the work in more than others — there is no hard and fast rule about this, but generally speaking I have found that small all-over designs make less difference to the size (compared with stocking stitch) than do large motifs. But there is really only one way to make sure — make tension squares. (You can cheat a little by making one fair isle tension square do for a number of similar designs, and you will probably get away with it). Of course, if part of your garment is to be in fair isle, and part in stocking stitch, then you must do tension squares for both fair isle and stocking stitch.

The only time I break the 'make a tension square' rule is that I do not normally make squares for ribbed welts or cuffs. I very quickly learned — as you will — how many stitch sizes smaller to use for ribbing or mock ribbing. If in doubt, try it out — but you will soon get the 'feeling' that enables you to judge correctly. As a rough guide, I like to work with a tension three whole sizes (sizes, not points) tighter for rib than for plain stocking stitch. (This refers to single bed work). With double bed or ribbing attachment rib the rule is not quite as simple and clear, and sometimes it pays to have slightly different stitch sizes on the front and back bed. But if you study patterns for your particular machine you will quickly build up a background of knowledge. And — golden rule — you can always try it out, if you are not sure.

This is yet another advantage of machine knitting: to try something out in hand knitting takes a long time, and it can really hurt to have to undo a piece of knitting that you have formed stitch by stitch. Machine knitting is so quick and easy that it is practically painless to knit, rip back, rewind, and knit again.

I have described one simple and reliable way of making tension squares. But there are other ways — you may prefer one of them.

Some knitters prefer to make much larger tension squares — over 6″ (15 cm) or 8″ (20 cm). You can do this simply by multiplying the number of stitches and rows.The larger the tension square (within reason) the more exact will be the measurements you obtain from it.

Owners of the Passap Duomatic will have, in their instruction book, a chart based on 100 stitches and 100 rows. This is a good method for this machine — I always use it with my Duomatic.

(NOTE: owners of double bed machines sometimes get confused as to how to count the number of stitches. When both beds have the needles set up in the same way — e.g. when both front and back bed have every needle, or every other needle, in working position — it is easy. If you have 50 stitches on the front bed, and 50 stitches on the back bed, then you are working with 100 stitches. Unfortunately patterns written for double bed machines do not always make this clear — nor do they always make it clear whether the needle set-up should be every needle or every other needle. Experience will soon teach you — in the early stages, you may have to try it out. But it is more complicated when the needle settings are irregular. This is rather unscientific, but quite soon after I began to knit (I started with a double bed machine) I worked out a very simple solution: I count only the stitches on the main bed (by which I mean the bed that has the most needles in working position). When shaping, I increase or decrease on the 'other bed' as the pattern requires. But for working out the tension, I count only the stitches on the main bed. Nowadays, some double bed patterns tell knitters to do this.)

In my first example, I assumed that you wanted to achieve a particular tension — in this case 26 stitches and 34 rows to the 4″ (10 cm) square. If and when you start to work from a Knit Radar (or other charting device) — see end of chapter — rather than from written patterns, you will find slightly different instructions for making a tension square (these are included with the charting device). With the Radar, you are not tied to any particular tension — all you need is to find which stitch size gives attractive results with the yarn you are using, and how many stitches and rows will give you the required 4″ (10 cm) square.

For instance, if you have a Knitmaster 323, you will find in your accessories box a short green ruler which I find invaluable. You knit your tension square — following the instruction book — and then you simply measure. There is one scale for the stitches and another for the rows, and the ruler gives you the number of stitches and rows to the 4″ (10 cm) square. This is based on a tension piece of 40 stitches and 60 rows.

Some knitters, after they have knitted a few inches in waste yarn, like to transfer the 21st needle, counting from each side of the centre) to the 22nd needle, push the two 21st needles back into non-working position, and leave them there. Then knit the 60 rows in main yarn, and change to contrast (this is when knitting 40 stitches and 60 rows for a tension piece).

The centre 40 stitches (20 each side of the centre mark) are clearly outlined by the ladder formed by leaving the two needles in non-working position. This is a good method for stocking stitch (it is not always satisfactory with stitch patterns) because it means you can measure anywhere you like across the knitting, and not only between the two stitches which have been marked with contrast wool — and it is obviously an advantage to measure in more than one place. Also, it avoids the possibility of the contrast yarn being pulled off the marked needles — and I think it is quicker, too.

Some knitters do not use contrast yarn — they knit the whole piece with their main yarn, but mark the beginning and the end of the 60 rows by knitting the row before and after on a very loose tension.

Making tension squares takes a little time (but it is well worth it) and as they should rest before being washed or pressed and measured, it is a good idea to make them beforehand. If you knit regularly, get into the habit of knitting tomorrow's tension squares at the end of today's knitting session. Or you may decide it would be even better to knit the tension pieces for your next half-dozen garments, all at once. This saves time because you need have only one washing/pressing session, instead of six.

However you knit your tension pieces, it is obvious that you should write down all the information you gain from them. I keep a tension notebook — I write down the stitch size I used, the measurements I obtained, the stitch pattern — and I then stick a small piece of the yarn I used on to the page, with a tiny square of sellotape. But when I do a tension square that I think is particularly attractive — that gives me all kinds of ideas for garments and/or furnishing fabrics — then I drop this square into a box I keep for the purpose (I have previously labelled it with details of yarn, stitch size, stitch pattern etc).

Some knitters like to knit in some of the information (rather like Madame Defarge at the guillotine, but this is pleasanter information). If they are working at stitch size 7, then near the beginning of the tension piece they make seven holes (by transferring seven stitches on to adjacent needles — just like a picot edge). If they are using — say — 7..., then they make their seven holes, miss a few stitches and make two holes. Of course they still have to record (and pin securely to the tension piece) information about the yarn and the measurement.

By keeping a careful record like this, you will find that as time goes on you need make fewer and fewer tension squares. This is particularly important with coned synthetics, where the tensions may not be standard ones, and where (if you buy odd lots) you can have such a variety of thicknesses and textures. If you always keep a piece of the yarn — either a short end taped to the page of the notebook, or the whole tension piece — then you can usually determine whether or not a new cone is of the same thickness and texture, and whether the tension squares you have already made will do for this new lot of yarn.

New knitters get rather worried when they find a pattern they would like to knit, but cannot obtain (or afford in some cases) the specified yarn. They are quite happy to substitute when the pattern says 'Blank's 4-ply'. But if a trade name is used — such as 'Blank's Juanita' — they are at a loss. They very often write to the publishers of machine knitting patterns and ask them always to state whether a yarn is 3-ply, 4-ply, double knit etc.

The publishers cannot always do this. In the first place, they have had this pattern designed for one specific yarn, and cannot be expected to take responsibility for the results if another yarn is used. And in the second place, many of these fancy yarns do not fall exactly into any of the standard categories. Some of them are in-between thicknesses — and in some cases the texture makes a difference, too.

However, there are clues, to help those who want to substitute another yarn.

If the pattern is written especially for your machine, then it will probably give a stitch size — and you will probably know that your particular machine tends to need a stitch size one point higher, or lower, than usually given in the patterns. This in itself is some guidance.

For example — if I see a pattern in Blank's 'Juanita' written for the Knitmaster 323, and the stitch size suggested is 7, then I know it will not be a fine yarn (such as 2-ply) and it will not be a double knit. Judging by past experience it is more likely to be a 4-ply. This does not tell me *exactly* what I want to know (i.e. it does not give me the name of a yarn I can substitute) but it narrows the field a good deal.

If the pattern is not written for a machine that I use, then I look at the number of stitches and rows to the 4" (10 cm) square — and obtain the same kind of information from these facts. For example — if the tension given is around 28 stitches and 40 rows, it is pretty sure to be roughly the equivalent of a 4-ply.

Next, I look very carefully at the illustration of the garment. If I can see that it is a tweedy wool, or a bouclé type, or a silky rayon-type — my search is still further narrowed down. Even if I cannot see details like this in the illustration, I can still learn a lot: if the garment is a tailored jacket, I know I must look for a nice firm yarn — possibly a crêpe; if it is a slinky negligée, then I need something soft that will drape beautifully.

By now, I have enough information to enable me to look through my stock of yarns and decide on one or possibly more that MIGHT be suitable. Then I try it (them) out. This is the only way to be sure. But at least, by doing a little preliminary detective work, I have not had to try everything from a firm double knit down to a fine coned synthetic. (Though remember that the fine coned yarns may often be the answer to this particular problem — because you can use two, three or more strands together; you can mix a strand of fine bouclé with a smooth synthetic, you can add a strand of fine industrial Lurex-type yarn — in short you can make your own yarns, as well as your own garments.)

Even when they are convinced of the value of tension squares, some knitters sometimes skip this chore, making thrift, and shortage of time, the excuse. They forget that if they don't get the tension right, before they start knitting, they may have to undo the garment, which will waste even more time. And that if they simply go ahead and make up a garment that is not the right size, it will not be a success, which is a terrible waste of money.

But — apart from their value in giving information — tension squares need not be wasted.

I strongly advise keeping some unusually attractive tension squares to refer to (and to show prospective customers, if you mean to knit for profit). But others — once you have recorded all the information — can be unravelled and used in making the garment. If you use this yarn for the inside of welts and cuffs you need not (usually) even wash or steam. Simply rewind into a ball and re-knit.

You can also use tension squares for small gifts — spectacle cases, purses, dolls' clothes, potholders. You can use knitted tension squares just as you do crochet motifs — make them into blankets, shawls, ponchos, cushion covers, shopping bags, shoulder bags, hold-alls, duffle bags, tea cosies, coffee cosies, kimonos, rugs, bedspreads.

If you prefer you can make tension squares larger than normal — large enough for a cushion cover or shoulder bag, for instance. As long as you mark (with thread or waste yarn that can be pulled out) the boundaries of your tension square, and record the information, the larger squares can go on to lead useful lives of their own.

Tension squares would not be wasted, even if you had to leave them just as they are, lying in a box, because without them you cannot knit to correct size. But with so many ways of using them — in addition to unravelling and re-using the wool for the garment — there is no excuse whatever for forgetting that CORRECT TENSION IS THE BASIS OF GOOD KNITTING.

Tension is important not only to enable us to follow correctly a printed pattern: it is just as vital when we want to design our own garments, which is not difficult, once we feel confident with the machine.

And there are two excellent devices — the Knit Radar (for Knitmaster machines) and the Knit Leader (for Jones machines) that make pattern designing really easy, and enable the average knitter to take advantage of all the wonderful things her machine is capable of.

I shall be talking about these two devices — and about designing simple garments and adapting printed patterns — in the next chapter.

12
All the Patterns you need

Many would-be machine knitters are discouraged from buying a machine because they believe that there are few machine knitting patterns available, and that these are either dull or way-out.

This is not true.

If you buy a machine by one of the makers I have already mentioned in this book, you will find (again the order is strictly alphabetical)
Jones produce their magazine *Stitchin' Time* — usually five times a year.
Knitmaster have their monthly magazine *Modern Knitting.*
Passap bring out model books — usually twice a year.
In addition to this, enquire about any booklets or leaflets which these manufacturers may have (simple patterns can usually be used with any machine).

I strongly advise any knitter to subscribe to the publication brought out by the makers of her machine. In my view it is money well spent. You may not wish to use the patterns in exactly the form shown, but you can learn a great deal about the possibilities of your machine by studying the publication which caters for that particular machine. I also think it is well worth subscribing to 'rival' publications. As you gain experience, you will see that many patterns — designed for other machines — can in fact be used with your machine (possibly with slight alterations). And if you cannot actually use the pattern, you may pick up all sorts of interesting ideas and — using the diagrams which most machine knitting patterns now include — you will soon be able *very easily* to design a similar pattern for use on your own machine.

Knitters with some of the simpler machines may feel rather left out — as they may feel their needs are not really catered for. However, they can use all the simple patterns (I shall be mentioning a good many sources in this chapter) and they can learn to design — and adapt — patterns just as easily as owners of more sophisticated machines. (And if the simple machine is a Knitmaster model 250 they can use the Knit

Radar; if it is a Jones 585 or 588 they can use the Knit Leader. (See page 95.) The monthly magazine *Home Sewing and Knitting* usually has one machine knitting pattern in each issue, and these are generally simple designs which can be used on any machine. The monthly *Pins and Needles* sometimes has machine knitting patterns, and occasionally they can be found in other magazines (e.g.*Living*).

If you have a Passap Duomatic machine, you should certainly get Mary Weaver's book *The Passap Duomatic* — enquire from Mary Weaver.

If you have a Knitmaster 321 or 323 *with ribbing attachment*, you should have Mary Weaver's *The Ribbing Attachment* — Part I and Part II — enquire as above.

These are the best knitting machine books I know — written clearly and simply from a wealth of actual experience. They contain plenty of attractive patterns, in yarns which are not difficult to obtain. These books are worth their weight in gold to the keen knitter — but they refer specifically to the machines named, not to knitting machines generally. It is to be hoped that Mary Weaver will soon be bringing out more books!

Patons and Baldwins have published a number of good clear machine knitting pattern books — and there are more in preparation. These are reliable basic patterns — the sort of thing that a new knitter needs if she is to gain experience and confidence; they are good plain styles that can be adapted and altered and used again and again, to produce a wide range of beautiful knitwear.

Some of the mail order firms can supply books of machine knitting patterns — enquire about this when you send for shade cards.

If you were confined to just these sources you would have all the patterns that any knitter could reasonably want. But there are plenty of other possibilities.

I have already talked in detail about *Cut-and-Sew* — see Chapter Nine. This makes it quite easy to work from a number of simple knitting or dressmaking patterns, and make any alterations you like — changing the neckline, the sleeves, the shoulder line etc.

And it is not difficult to alter simple patterns to suit your own individual size, shape or wishes and shape these as you knit. Once you start to do this, you are on the way to designing your own knitwear.

Probably your first attempt at 'designing' will be a minor alteration to an existing pattern. Say that this pattern gives you a side seam of 13″ (32.5 cm), but you are knitting for a tall friend and want the side seam to be 16″ (40 cm). Your tension square tells you that there are 10 rows to the inch (2.5 cm), you need three extra inches (7.5 cm), so you knit 30 extra rows.

This couldn't be easier, even for a beginner.

But perhaps it is the sleeve that has to be — say — 2″ (5 cm) longer. And the sleeve is not knitted straight, as the front and back of the sweater were, but with increases. If you simply add the extra 20 rows, where will these go? At the beginning or at the end? In either case you will have a straight piece of knitting, preceded or followed by the shaped portion of the sleeve, and this may not look right. (Of course, some sleeves are knitted straight — in this case simply add the extra rows. But I am assuming this is a classic sweater where the sleeve is wider at the top than at the cuff.)

To make a nice smooth slope you have to 'feed' those extra 20 rows in gradually. Use the method I have described in Chapter Ten (sleeve head).

The same principle applies to lengthening or shortening skirt panels — or any shaped piece of knitting.

It is just as easy to make *small* adjustments in width. You are using a 34″ (85 cm) pattern, but want to make it 1″ (2.5 cm) more round the bust. This means you need add only ½″ (1.25 cm) to front and ½″ (1.25 cm) to the back — which gives you the extra inch (2.5 cm). If your tension is 6 stitches to the inch (2.5 cm), then you need add only 3 stitches to front and 3 stitches to back. Cast on with the extra 3 stitches, knit as the pattern, remembering that you will always have 3 more stitches than the pattern says, and when you come to neck and shoulder shaping, add one extra stitch to each shoulder and one to the neck. This will not spoil the line of the pattern but the 6 extra stitches (3 back and 3 front) will give you the extra inch (2.5 cm) you need. You can use this method when the number of extra stitches is slightly more — say you need an extra 6 stitches on front *and* back (12 stitches altogether, to give you an extra 2″ (5 cm)) then 2 extra stitches on each shoulder and 2 extra stitches on the neck will still not spoil your pattern. But don't — until you are more experienced — try making pattern alterations of more than about 2″ (5 cm). If you do, you may run into problems with sleeve and armhole shapings. It can be done — quite easily — but not by a complete beginner. Start with very simple alterations, and you will soon be able to tackle more complicated ones.

If the only alteration you need is a slightly deeper (or shorter) armhole, then you can knit more (or fewer) rows, on the straight, before reaching the shoulder, and then increase/decrease the height of the sleeve head to correspond. I have explained how to do this in Chapter Ten. Remember that generally the height of the sleeve head is around two-thirds of the depth of the armhole, so if you add — say — 6 rows to the armhole, then you will need to add 4 rows to the sleeve head.

I don't advise anyone except an experienced knitter or dressmaker to alter either armholes or sleeve heads by more than a very small amount. It is usually safe to make small adjustments — following the suggestions I have given. But remember that alterations at this point can make a great difference to the way a garment looks and feels. It is tempting to think that a really deep armhole, with a taller sleeve head and more width across the upper part of the sleeve, will give a lovely easy-fitting, good-looking garment. But while *just a little* extra ease can improve a garment for some figures, too much can be disastrous. What inexperienced knitters sometimes forget is that if you start shaping the armhole much lower than on the original pattern, then you 'steal' width from the bust/chest area, and if this is too tight, the garment will look terrible and be most uncomfortable to wear.

I have thought about this problem a lot, because I am one of the knitters who feel that standard patterns make armholes and sleeves rather narrow. I often add *a little* ease, and am pleased. I have sometimes added too much — and been very disappointed. It seems to me that the answer — for those of us who like lots of roomy freedom — is batwing, dolman, square armhole or dropped shoulder line. I find all these shapes really attractive and wearable in knitwear, and one or other of them is usually in fashion (as I write, the dropped shoulder line is very popular). A well-shaped raglan also gives more ease round the armhole and upper arm than most classic set-in sleeves.

Not many of us conform absolutely to standard measurements — we may look 'normal' but in fact most of us are slightly taller or shorter, or narrower or wider than standard measurements — so it is very likely that if you knit for yourself and your family and friends you will quite soon start making this kind of minor alteration. It is good that you should — because it shows you clearly that there is nothing mysterious about knitting patterns, and that even a beginner can make small alterations without disaster (it also shows you that if you do make a mistake, with machine knitting it is no great hardship to have to undo and re-knit). But there is no reason why you should make more than a very few mistakes — work things out carefully on paper, draw diagrams to help you, and you will soon gain confidence.

One idea usually sparks off another. And another, and another . . . So once you have made even a simple alteration to a pattern, there will probably be no holding you. You will realise that you need never again put up with knitwear that is not just right for you: you won't need to tuck up too-long sweaters, or tug down too-short ones, or wriggle in uncomfortably tight sleeves or armholes, or keep pushing back cuffs that slip over your hands. You will also see that you can do more than simply make your knitwear fit. You can change the appearance of a simple basic pattern so that having the right clothes for every occasion becomes easier and cheaper than you dreamed it could be.

From here it is an easy step to designing your own patterns.

This book is not for the knitter who intends to become a professional designer. There are courses of study, and technical books, for serious students. All I want to do is help the amateur knitter who wants to make lovely clothes for herself and her family (and perhaps for sale too) as easily and quickly as possible — the knitter who does not always find what she wants in the magazines or pattern books.

So I am not going to say very much about 'classic' raglan and set-in sleeve garments, because there is no shortage of such patterns (even if you have to adapt them slightly to get a perfect fit). But sometimes you see something in a magazine, or in an expensive boutique, or an actress in a play is wearing something you know you'd look good in, too. And then, quite often, there is no pattern. This is where the ability to design your own is really useful.

I am not a designer, but I can — and do — 'design' my own knitted garments with a good deal of success. I am sure you can do the same (or better) and so I am going to tell you about one of my favourite patterns, and just how I worked it out, and how adaptable and useful it is.

In the early days of the dropped shoulder line I could not find a knitting pattern for this style, but I very much wanted such a jacket. It was easy to see — by looking at the ready-made jackets in expensive shops and by studying dressmaking patterns — that the shape was very simple indeed — like this.

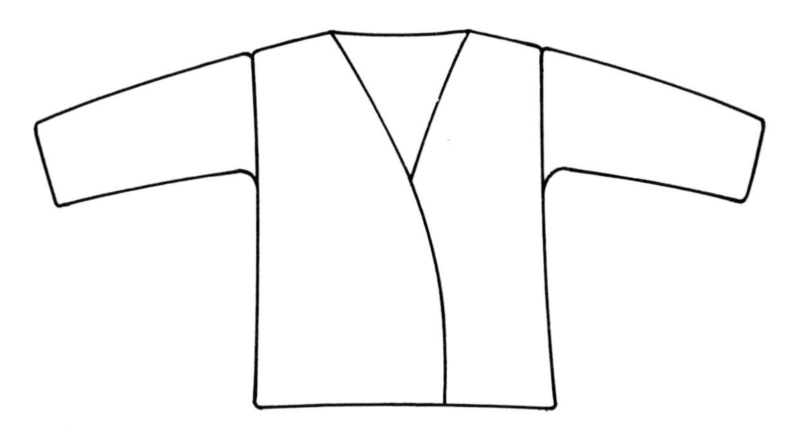

I drew out the shapes, put in the measurements that suited me, and then all I had to do was work out the number of stitches and rows I should need (I have already described how to do this).

This is the actual pattern I worked out: (the yarn was coned Shetland).

Stitch size: 7 (on the Knitmaster 323); this gave me a tension of 29½ stitches and 43 rows to the 4″ square (10 cm).

Back: I cast on 158 stitches. Made a hem by knitting 17 rows at T. 5, 1 row at T. 8, put the row counter to 0, worked 17 rows at T. 6, then changed to T. 7 and worked straight until the row counter showed 284.

I decided I wanted 40 stitches for the back of the neck (I like garments to fit snugly here — you may wish to make the back neck wider. Just measure). 158 stitches - 40 = 118 stitches. Divide these in two for shoulders = 59 stitches each shoulder. I sloped the shoulders by putting into holding position 12 stitches each end 4 times (48 stitches each shoulder) and then 11 stitches each end (59 stitches each shoulder).

After finishing the shaping, I knitted one row over all stitches (working one shoulder at a time) and stripped off with waste yarn. I then knitted a few rows with waste yarn over the 40 stitches for the neck (to save casting off I just ran a thread through the last row knitted in main yarn, as this was concealed when the double band was sewn on. If you prefer, you can cast off — I do this when I use a ribbed (single thickness) band instead of a doubled stocking stitch band).

Fronts: 78 stitches each. Make hem same as back. Work straight till RC 174 then turn RC back to 0.

I had to reduce 78 stitches to 59 (shoulder) in 110 rows — this worked out like this:

decrease 1 stitch at neck edge every 6 rows 15 times (90 rows worked, 63 stitches remain). Decrease 1 stitch every 5 rows 4 times — (110 rows worked, 59 stitches remain). 110 rows plus the 174 already worked (before I put the row counter back to 0) = 284, which is the same as the back. I shaped the shoulders as back.

Sleeves: 150 stitches (this time I worked a band of fair isle on the hem, but this is optional). Knit straight for 110 rows — strip off with waste yarn. If you prefer you can cast off, or you can pick up the stitches for the sleeve and knit downwards.

Pocket: 42 stitches and 70 rows — with a fair isle band (to match cuff) on the top. I sewed this pocket neatly into position and it looked excellent. But nowadays I usually make a larger pocket and I very often use one of the alternative methods I have described in Chapter Fourteen, especially the 'buttonhole' pocket.

Front band: 34 stitches — knitted until long enough to go right round both fronts and back of neck. I machined this into position (right sides facing) and then slip stitched to the inside. Nowadays I quite often make a ribbed band.

Belt: I made this in ribbing — long enough to tie. It can also be made in stocking stitch (seamed — by machine — down the long sides) or in tubular.

The yarn cost me 8p an ounce (28.35 gm) (I bought it from a market stall) and the garment took 22 oz (623.7 gm) — so total cost was £1.76. The week after I had finished it, I was in London, made a point of looking at similar jackets, and found they were selling for £10-£12. (Since then, like everything else, they have gone up.)

This casual wrap-over jacket fits me beautifully (I am size 34″ - 85 cm) and looks good either over a thin blouse or sweater or over quite a bulky garment. I have made the identical jacket for a friend who is size 36″ (90 cm) and it is right for her, too. A friend who is size 38″ (95 cm) tried mine on and asked for one *exactly like it* because she likes her jackets edge-to-edge. But if she had wanted it to wrap over, I could very easily have added a couple of inches. It is just as simple to alter the length, for anyone exceptionally tall or short. No need to alter front shapings — simply knit more, or fewer, rows on the straight before starting the front slope. Sleeves, too, can be made longer or shorter to suit individual wishes.

I have now knitted this jacket more times than I can remember — for myself, for friends, to make money for charity. Using the same basic shapes (but of course working out the number of stitches and rows each time I tried a different yarn) I have made it in Shetland, botany, crêpe, good quality synthetics. These were all roughly 4-ply equivalents, but I have also made it in double knitting — plain and tweed and random, and I have just finished one that is made with two strands of coned Shetland. This Shetland is roughly 4-ply equivalent, so two strands together make a really warm, hard-wearing jacket — I made this on my Knitmaster 323, using tension 9 and every other needle.

I vary the pockets, vary the fair isle designs, sometimes do a border of fair isle round the bottom as well as on cuffs and pocket tops. I sometimes use all-over fair isle, with plain bands, belt, pocket tops and cuffs. One — made in Argyll coned 'Ferntex' (plain brown with a random orange/yellow/white) — was a sensation at a bazaar.

I have adapted the pattern to make some very attractive over-blouses. Front and back same width, back neck scooped out just 1″ (2.5 cm), front neck scooped out from 3″ (7.5 cm) to 6″ (15 cm) according to taste, and finished with a narrow band of stocking stitch, rib, mock rib (stripes or fair isle can be incorporated if wished). I add two pockets and a belt. The neck shaping is easy to do — if you have come this far with your knitting it shouldn't worry you at all, but of course you can cut-and-sew if you prefer. Or you can knit straight up to the top and do a slit neckline — very popular now. These tops look wonderful, worn with a shirt or thin sweater and trousers. Or with a matching knitted or woven skirt you have a good looking suit at very low cost.

I still haven't exhausted the possibilities of this very simple pattern. Here are some of the things I intend to do:

make it in a thick yarn, in an all-over tuck pattern, to give an Aran effect;
make it in slip stitch, for a light but firm fabric;
make it in weaving, with skirt to match;
make it longer, for a warm dressing gown;
make it shorter, in a soft fine wool, for a bedjacket;
make full length sleeves, either to hang loose or to gather into ribbed cuffs;
make it in a thick tweedy wool and trim with fur fabric collar and cuffs;
make it in lurex-type yarn for evening wear (this could have lightweight fur fabric trimming, too — a band of 'fur' right round front edges, bottom of jacket, and cuffs, with the jacket left hanging loose, would be luxurious).

This pattern is a treasure to me — I hope it will be just as useful to you.

As well as providing you with the garment you want — and innumerable variations — your very own basic pattern, whether it is similar to mine or not, will do a lot for you if you are a fairly new knitter. It will show you, once and for all, how very simple most knitted shapes are, especially with today's fashions. If you look in shops that sell top quality knitwear, or study the fashion magazines, you will see that the best knitteds are essentially simple. Too much detail spoils the effect, and it is line, colour, texture and *beautiful, painstaking finish* that gives the luxury look.

Once you begin to see what makes good knitwear tick, you will gain confidence to take liberties with the professionals' patterns. Don't alter for the sake of altering — no reason not to take advantage of the professionals' brilliance *when* they give you what you want. But once you have learned a little about designing, you do not need to accept, slavishly, everything that the experts suggest. If we like something, but feel we'd like it even better with a different neckline or some other alteration, then we can make that change. I love many of the designs featured in knitting machine manufacturers' publications, but this does not mean that I always knit them exactly as they appear in the book. I see something I like the look of, and I interpret it to suit myself.

In a good many years of altering, adapting and sometimes designing, I have found that:

(*1*) Sleeve heads and armholes are the tricky bits, when it comes to making alterations. Until you are experienced, don't attempt more than small changes (I have talked about this already).

(*2*) If I come to a shape — usually a curve — that is difficult to translate into stitches and rows, I draw the shape out and mark it off into small sections, which are much easier to handle than the whole thing. You can, if you wish, draw the shape on squared paper and mark these squares to match your tension. For instance, if you are using inch-squared paper, and your tension is 7 stitches and 10 rows, then mark the paper so that each square is divided into 7 sections across and 10 sections down. This shows you exactly the number of stitches you should have on each row. This is fiddly — but could be worth doing if you feel timid. You will soon gain confidence and realise you can manage without so much painstaking preparation.

(*3*) Cut-and-sew plays a big part in (my sort of) designing. It makes it possible to alter — say — a neckline after the garment has been tried on. It also means that curved edges that will be bound (such as on ponchos and capes) can be knitted straight, or roughly to shape, and then marked, stitched and cut.

(*4*) It is very important to make sure that the yarn is suitable for the garment. It is easy to get carried away by a lovely colour or interesting texture, and try to make a full length coat or long skirt in a knitted fabric that is too soft to hang well, or a hostess gown in a fabric that is too stiff to drape and flow. If in doubt, make your tension square twice as large as usual, then handle it, look at it carefully, use your imagination and 'see' the finished garment. Trying to make a yarn do a job it is not suitable for is a great time-waster, and very frustrating for inexperienced knitters. This was my Number One mistake when I was new to machine knitting. I don't suppose any of us would be silly enough to buy chiffon to make a tailored suit — but some of us do equally ridiculous things with yarns.

The sort of 'designing' I have been talking about is not likely to result in your having your own collection, that the fashion buyers of the world will flock to — though it could be the first step on a road that leads there. But it will give you satisfaction, and enable you to knit almost anything you want to knit.

Designing can be even easier than this. For those of us whose time is limited, and who want to turn out as many garments — in as many different styles and sizes — as possible, in as short a time as possible, there is very good news.

The Knit Radar (for Knitmaster machines) and the Knit Leader (for Jones machines) have revolutionised (over-worked word, but in this case it is justified) machine knitting.

Both manufacturers have literature about these wonderful

You can't get away from uni-sex. And in knitwear, it's a good thing; many mothers deliberately choose designs that look good on girls and boys, so that garments can be handed down. And cosy, casual jackets like these are ideal off-duty wear for young and not-so-young couples. These jackets are very like my favourite pattern which is described on page 91.

accessories, so it would be a waste of space for me to repeat that information here. Contact the manufacturer of your machine, or your local stockist, and study the leaflet.

I use my Knit Radar (Knitmaster) nearly all the time. This does not imply a criticism of the Knit Leader (Jones) — it is simply because I use my Knitmaster 323 more than any other machine.

The Knit Radar has speeded up my knitting enormously. Like many women, I have to knit mainly in the evenings and sometimes, by then, I am tired and look forward to 'a nice knit' as a relaxation. It is not difficult to work out a pattern, with paper and pencil, but it can be just a little daunting at the end of a long day at your desk.

With the Knit Radar all I need is the shape I want to knit, and a carefully measured tension square. The Knit Radar shows me how many stitches to cast on, how many rows to knit, where to increase and decrease . . . I am independent of the written pattern. When I have a shape I like, I can knit it in stocking stitch, fair isle, lace stitch, tuck stitch, weaving — in any type of yarn (subject to rules of common sense and suitability) without having to work out a pattern.

Both the Knit Radar and Knit Leader are supplied with a set of basic designs. Additional material is available, and as this is added to from time to time, you should contact manufacturer or stockist for-up-to date news. And of course you can draw your own shapes: you can use the diagrams in magazines, or simple dressmaking patterns, or copy a favourite garment.

And there is another advantage that not all knitters realise. If you find a knitting pattern without a diagram, and you would like to make this but cannot achieve the tension given, you can use your Knit Radar to draw a diagram of the pattern. Set your Knit Radar to the number of rows and stitches per 4″ (10 cm) square given in the pattern you want to copy. Put in a blank sheet of paper the same size and shape as one of the basic blocks that come with the Knit Radar. Then read off the number of stitches you would have to cast on, and turn the feeding dial one movement at a time — just as if it were being moved up by the movement of the cam box, as you knit. You can then read off, for each row, how many stitches there should be, and if you mark these points on the paper (with a pencil) you will have a dot-to-dot outline of the shape of the garment. And this shape is all you need to work with the Knit Radar — join up the dots and use the outline as if it were one of your basic blocks. This can quite often be used with hand as well as machine knitting patterns.

I have already said that both the Knit Radar and the Knit Leader are supplied with clear instructions. All the same, I must tell you that I have heard from a number of knitters — intelligent people — who find these attachments difficult to use — in fact one excellent knitter told me she 'couldn't get the hang of the thing at all'.

Because of this I have (although I was already familiar with them) gone through both instruction books again. And I cannot honestly see that they could be improved upon, or made clearer. If you are one of the few knitters who are having difficulty with your charting attachment, I would like to assure you that the instructions *are* correct, and the device *does* work. I make this point because whenever I am baffled by anything mechanical my immediate reaction is to think that either the instruction book or the device itself is at fault. I should so much like knitters to realise the great advantage of this accessory, so I am mentioning a few possible causes of disappointment, in the hope that one of these may be your problem.

Tension — as with all knitting — is absolutely basic to the successful use of a charting device. At a fashion show recently I talked to a knitter who said angrily that her Knit Radar was a waste of money, it didn't work etc., etc. I asked her if she was quite sure she had measured her tension square correctly and she replied: "Oh, I don't bother with tension squares. I always use a yarn that is roughly equivalent to 4-ply, so I know it will come up to about 7 stitches and 10 rows to the inch, and that's near enough for me . . ."

Well, it may be near enough for her, but it is NOT near enough for her poor misunderstood charting device. This is a mechanical device which can work only on the basis of what we human knitters 'tell' it. And if we 'tell' it that our yarn is going to have 28 stitches and 40 rows to the 4″ (10 cm) square which is 7 stitches and 10 rows to 1″ (2.5 cm) when in fact the yarn produces — say — 26 stitches and 41 rows to the 4″ (10 cm) square, *then the garment will not fit.* And this applies whether you use a Knit Radar or follow a printed pattern.

I have talked about this in great detail in Chapter Eleven. ALL responsible writers about machine knitting, ALL good instruction books, stress that unless you get the correct tension your garments will not come up to the required size, but many knitters still ignore this and think that guessing is good enough. It isn't. If you are one of those who feel disappointed in your Knit Radar, the most likely reason for your dissatisfaction is that you have not taken the trouble to measure the tension correctly.

Inserting the pattern sheet correctly is another essential that knitters sometimes skimp. Make quite sure it is lined up EXACTLY AS YOUR INSTRUCTION BOOK TELLS YOU. Just rolling it in and hoping for the best is not enough. You must also take care to position your stitch scale exactly.

Setting the row indicator correctly is — of course — also necessary. I met one knitter recently who was disappointed that her garments came up too long. When we discussed this, it came out that her sight is not good for close work and she had actually been setting the indicator wrongly. She bought a small magnifying glass and is now getting good results.

Following the right line on your pattern is another 'must', and though this too is obvious, I have known knitters to become confused when they get to the armhole shaping, where the lines outlining the various sizes are very close together. If this is your difficulty, then trace off just one size at a time. Or you can make yourself a multi-size tracing, but use a different coloured pen for each size, or indicate the different sizes with different lines — e.g. solid, dot-dash, dotted.

Before we leave the Knit Radar, I should like to pass on a few hints that I have learned since I began to use mine regularly.

(*1*) When I need to cast off a number of stitches on each side of the work — e.g. for armhole shaping — I find it easier to cast off — say — 6 stitches on the right hand side (where the carriage is) using the yarn in the yarn feeder, and then — using a length of matching yarn — cast off the required number of stitches on the other side. This means I need stop only once instead of twice. This is a very tiny saving in time, but when you are knitting a number of garments, each of which has several 'steps' in the shaping, it is worth while.

(*2*) Slight alterations to a garment can be made simply by changing the stitch scale in your Knit Radar (leaving stitch size on the machine the same). A clever knitter who regularly earns with her machine drew my attention to this. We had been talking about how standard armholes and sleeves are sometimes too tight for some people, especially in jackets or cardigans that may be worn over quite bulky garments. We discussed various ideas — and later tried them out and compared notes: using the sleeves from the next size; working an extra 4—6 rows on the straight part of each armhole (i.e. after shaping is completed), then adding 4 rows to the sleeve cap (working these in as convenient). We then found that to make the sleeve *just a little* wider all we had to do was to alter the stitch scale to the scale two numbers higher. One pattern we use a lot calls for the stitch scale that gives 28 stitches to 4" (10 cm); when we wanted to make the sleeves a little wider we changed it for the scale that gives 30 stitches to the 4" (10 cm) square. We knitted the sleeve in just the same way, and we did not change the actual stitch size on the machine.

Think about this. Say your original sleeve measured 16" (40 cm) across the widest part. According to stitch scale for 28 sts = 4" (10 cm) that would give 112 stitches. Change the stitch scale to 30, and you would have 120 stitches — this would allow a good inch (2.5 cm) extra for added ease.

We have both done this repeatedly and been pleased with the results. So far we have always been working with a 4-ply yarn. If you were using a very thick, or very fine, yarn you might have to make a smaller or larger adjustment. But the principle would remain the same.

You could make a similar small alteration by changing the number on the row indicator. But usually it is so simple to alter length that I don't think this would often be necessary.

Remember that if you wish to shape a waist by changing to a smaller stitch *size*, then you should leave the stitch *scale* as it is. Before starting to knit a garment where you intend to shape the waist in this way, do a tension check and find out how many rows to 4" (10 cm) there will be *on the smaller stitch size* (as well as with main tension) and adjust your row indicator *for this section only*, remembering to turn back to the previous number on the row indicator as soon as the waist section is finished.

Example: you are working at a tension — say 6 — that gives 40 rows = 10 cm. But you want to do just the waist section (say 2" - 5 cm) with a smaller stitch size (say 5) to pull it in slightly. If using stitch size 5, instead of 6, means that 44 rows = 4" (10 cm) (instead of 40 rows) then you must change the row indicator from 40 to 44 for the waist section only.

(3) The Knit Radar and the basic patterns supplied are intended to help you, not to tyrannise over you! ! I have met several knitters who felt that once having bought a Knit Radar and learned to use it, they MUST use it all the time. Now most of the time the Knit Radar — in my view — is a great time and trouble saver, and real value for money. But there are times when you can do better without it. For instance, if I am shaping a raglan, I know how many rows I need, I know how many stitches I need to decrease, and very often (I don't say always) it is simpler just to work out how many rows there will be between each decrease, and knit away without botherng to glance either at the Knit Radar or a printed pattern. But I have talked to knitters who feel vaguely guilty if they do this.

The basic patterns should be treated in just the same way (I am referring to those which come with the Knit Radar — the Knitmaster basic pattern system which is an optional extra shows in detail how to adapt the various patterns). Several knitters have written to me and complained that the patterns supplied with the Radar are "no good for our family because we are all extra tall". But it is so simple to make the garments longer. You can either simply knit the extra length before you start on the pattern proper — estimating the number of rows you will need — or you can extend the side seams of the pattern and draw in a new hem line. Similarly you can change the neckline, make full sleeves, shape in at the waist, modify the slope of the shoulder: all you need do is take a pencil and draw in the outline you want, on the basic pattern. Or you can draw yourself a new pattern, using the basic as a guideline but incorporating any changes you want to make.

In my opinion it is very important for knitters to realise how easy it is to adapt the patterns that come with the Knit Radar, because as long as they believe they have to use this one set of shapes slavishly, they are not getting real value for money. The Knit Radar costs — as I write this — over £30, which is a lot of money for a 'gadget'. When it is used to its full extent — to make it possible for you to knit anything you like in the yarn and stitch pattern of your choice — it is money well spent. By all means start off cautiously (I did). But then go on to making small alterations to the patterns — just lengthening or shortening; then see how you can change the sleeves, the neckline etc; then start to make your own blocks, from diagram patterns or simple dressmaking patterns — or from your own designs. And *then*, I'm pretty sure, you will value your Knit Radar as much as I do, which is saying a great deal.

(*4*) Even after they feel very confident to vary the outlines of patterns, some knitters do not realise that the Knit Radar also makes it possible to position stripes, bands of fair isle, single motifs etc, faster and more easily than by working it out. Pencil these in lightly, so that you can rub them out later. (Remember you are working to half scale.)

Summing up this very long chapter, you can obtain patterns for your knitting machine by:

(*1*) Using the cut-and-sew method (see Chapter Nine).

(*2*) Using makers' publications, spinners' publications, women's magazines.

(*3*) Altering or adapting, to your own requirements, any of (*1*) or (*2*).

(*4*) Designing your own — start with something really simple and loose fitting (like my jacket) to give yourself confidence.

(*5*) Using one of the charting devices (such as Knit Radar).

Some of the perfectly good knitting machines that have spent the last few years at the back of a cupboard are there partly because the owners complained that they couldn't get the patterns they wanted.

I have tried to show that there are in fact more patterns available than the average knitter is likely to be able to use up in a long and busy life.

13
Yarns for your Knitting Machine

One of the reasons for buying a knitting machine is to make garments cheaply. But this does not mean using poor quality yarn.

I recently talked to a new machine knitter who was grumbling that her machine was a waste of money — the fabric it produced was harsh and stiff. I asked her to show me the yarn she was using, and found that it was like cheap string and shed whiskers and loose dye every time it was touched (she had bought it for 3p an ounce - 28.35 gm). I gave her an odd ball of soft coned synthetic, stood over her while she knitted it up, and of course she was surprised and delighted. I then showed her that although my yarn cost three times as much as hers, it was so economical that the price difference was almost wiped out — and as the cheap yarn didn't, in any case, produce a garment that anyone could have borne to wear, her 3p an ounce (28.35 gm) was a complete waste of money while my 9p an ounce (28.35 gm) produced a delightful garment for under £1.

Never use harsh coarse yarn on your knitting machine. It is horrible to knit, doesn't produce anything worth knitting, and may damage your machine.

Later, when you have gained experience and got the 'feel' of yarns, you will be able to have all the fun of tracking down bargains on market stalls and in 'job lots'. But while you are new to machine knitting, stick to yarns that other machine knitters have already proved to be good (and easy to knit).

If you are lucky enough to have a good machine knitting centre near you, go and ask their advice (I have given the names of a few centres in the Appendix on page 133. One of them does mail order.)

You can also buy good coned yarns (though they may be a little more expensive) from the knitting wool department of some of the big stores. Look out for Argyll, and for Hayfield, and by the time this book appears, Marriners may also have coned yarns available. All these are established firms that you can rely on.

And of course you can use many hand knitting yarns. It is a disadvantage to have to keep starting new balls, but nowadays hand-knitting yarns come in such a fascinating range of colours and types that no keen knitter could really bear to ignore them. Some of the 'fancy' yarns may be difficult to knit on the machine, and as new ones are constantly appearing, I cannot give a list of these. The only way is to buy just one ball — or beg an oddment from a hand-knitting friend, and try it out. Most good quality hand-knitting yarns, up to D.K., will knit beautifully by machine. And even yarns that are too thick to knit on every needle on most machines may produce beautiful knit-woven fabric, or knit on alternate needles. And some quite chunky wools will knit on the Knitmaster 250, which is designed to take thicker yarns.

Hand-knitting yarns I have found particularly good are listed in the Appendix on page 133.

Last, but not least, are the mail order firms. I have come across just a few that supply poor, harsh yarns, but there are many more that give real value for money. If you are unable to get to the shops, if you like to browse over shade cards and choose your yarns at home, if you like to have your customers choose their yarns for you to order — then a good mail order firm is a good friend. I have listed those that I know to be reliable in the Appendix on page 133.

There are two types of coned yarns — both of enormous benefit to the machine knitter — that need special handling.

Shetland Wool

on the cone looks dull, greasy and stringy, quite unlike the beautiful Shetland garments we see in expensive stores, or the Shetland yarn sold for hand knitting. Knit this unpromising looking wool on a tension that produces a rather loose fabric — almost 'holey' (as a very rough guide I use, on my Knitmaster 323, T. 7 for stocking stitch and around T. 8 for fair isle; I know other knitters who use slightly smaller stitch sizes). Then wash it, in fairly hot water and mild detergent (I like washing-up liquid for this first de-oiling wash). Rinse well, add a little fabric softener to the water (there are several good ones but I use Boots *Soft Rinse* because it comes in conveniently large containers). Press, with a hot iron and very damp cloth, when almost dry, and you will have a really beautiful firm, smooth, soft fabric, at small cost.

Not only the appearance but also the size of the knitting will be changed when it is washed, so there is no point in measuring a tension

It is always the unusual that costs more — IF you have to buy it ready-made. A dress, tunic and poncho set like this would be too expensive for many of us even to consider. Just buying suitable fabric and making our own would be costly. But when you knit, and weave, your own fabric (as you can with a knitting machine) and then make it into just the garments you want, top fashion outfits like this can be within the reach of most. Dress and tunic are knitted; poncho is woven, in beautiful muted colours, and looks like exclusive tweed. This outfit was made, by a clever amateur knitter, in some of the beautiful 'Silverknit' yarns.

square until after washing. This yarn can be bought from a good many knitting machine centres, and on market stalls (if you buy from a source you do not know, be careful not to buy the very fine 1-ply type, which is difficult). The most useful are 2/16 which knits up like 2-ply (you can use two strands together if you wish) and 2/8 which knits up like 4-ply.

Fine Coned Synthetics

I am not talking about the repeatable, 4-ply coned synthetics obtainable in stores etc, but of the very fine yarns which are really produced for industrial use, but can be a great blessing to the amateur machine knitter. These yarns are beautifully soft, they come in lovely colours, they are inexpensive, and they wash and wear well. But — usually — they have to be used two, three, four or even more strands together. This may worry a complete beginner (and don't forget I have already urged that beginners should start with a good quality 4-ply) but is perfectly simple once you have mastered your machine. Some knitters wind all the strands together, in a big ball; others prefer to knit from a number of cones. I prefer the latter way, but sometimes I have had to undo a piece of knitting, and find that it is perfectly easy to re-knit, using all the strands wound together.

These very fine yarns are not usually referred to as 3-ply, 4-ply etc, but come in various 'counts'. Although the 'count' is normally given on the inside of the cone, sometimes the yarn sold on market stalls or in job lots has been rewound on to other cones, and this may mislead beginners. It is a good idea, in the beginning, to buy your fine coned synthetics either from a knitting machine centre, or from a firm like Foster Yarn (see Appendix on page 133) so you know exactly what you are getting. Once you have gained experience, you will know what knits up nicely, and how many strands you should use. As a rough guide, I often use 2/30 yarn, two strands each of two different colours, in an all-over fair isle, at Tension 4 to Tension 5 (depending on how firm I want the fabric to be). But I have also knitted at Tension 3 with good results. When making stocking stitch garments in these fine yarns, I usually use two strands, at Tension 5 to Tension 6, or three strands at Tension 7 for a slightly heavier garment. All these tensions are given for my Knitmaster 323 (but remember your machine — even if it is the same model — may be slightly different).

These are only suggestions. The advantage of these fine yarns is that you can take as many strands as you wish, and experiment with tensions and stitch patterns, until you achieve the result you like. I know knitters who go on adding strands until they produce the equivalent of a soft, thick D.K.

You can also use these fine yarns to achieve lovely random effects — (see Chapter Three).

14
Is this your Problem?

The more you knit, the easier it becomes. Most of the things that seemed complicated will — one by one — suddenly become simple. But sometimes a few problems remain . . . "I can do everything but . . ." say so many letters, and I can remember my own early knitting days, when my heart used to sink whenever I was asked to make a garment with a collar, or pockets. I was pretty good at everything else, but collars and pockets spelled disaster.

Collars

This is not a book for the genius — who can start designing almost before her machine is unpacked — but for the average knitter (you and I) who wants to knit to a high standard, but wants to do it as easily as possible. I soon realised that I could learn to knit collars only by knitting collars, so I found a few good reliable patterns (you can do the same — see Chapter Twelve) with collars, and even if I was not going to knit the garment, I knitted the collar. I used oddments of yarn, but I knitted as carefully as if I was making a luxury garment. I labelled these collars — number of pattern, yarn used, stitch size etc etc — and put them into my collar box. By the time I had knitted (sometimes more than once) half-a-dozen collars, really taking care with both knitting and making up, and really examining what made the collar a success, I knew quite a lot about collars. I also found that when a friend wanted a garment "Just like this one, but with a collar . . ." I could almost always use one of the collars I was already familiar with. I might have to make it slightly longer or deeper, but essentially I could use the same collar again and again on different garments. I built up a repertoire of collar patterns. Whenever I saw a new one that I liked, I knitted it when I had a little spare time, and added it to my collection. If collars worry you, I suggest you do the same.

But even this does not solve all collar problems. Even the experts (the designers) are not infallible, and I sometimes found I could make small alterations that improved my garments.

(*a*) Some patterns give instructions for a ribbed band (on a V-neck cardigan) with a separate collar, also in rib, attached to the edge of the ribbed band. I found that I could usually get a better appearance by knitting the ribbed collar according to the pattern, transferring all stitches to one bed, knitting in stocking stitch for the depth of the band, stripping off with waste yarn, and attaching the last row of stocking stitch to the point where band joined cardigan.

(*b*) Sometimes ribbed collars — knitted according to a pattern — come off the machine with a 'pull' to one side, which means that the points do not lie in the same direction. Sometimes it is possible (with wool) to correct this by steaming and pressing, but even with pure wool, you can only press ribbing with great caution, and with synthetics it may not be advisable to press at all. I solve the problem by knitting the collar in two separate halves, and joining it down the centre back, which can be done almost invisibly. This gives two good edges and the points of the collar look the same.

(*c*) If you knit a ribbed collar lengthwise, the cast-on and the cast-off edges may not look identical. I start and finish with waste yarn, then take a wool needle and 'oversew' first the cast-on and then the cast-off stitches, pulling and easing gently until I have a nice smooth appearance very similar to an automatic cast-on.Practise this with odd pieces of knitting. Or knit a length of narrow ribbing (I like 4 stitches on the back bed and either 2 or 3 on the front) and knit until long enough to go round both short edges and one long edge of the collar. Flat stitched to the edge of the collar, and gently eased round the corners, this gives a neat finish. If you prefer, you need not knit a separate edging — cast on the number of stitches for the edging, knit until long enough to go along the short edge of the collar (if you are not quite sure about length, then you can start with waste yarn and adjust later), then cast on the stitches for the main collar (I always have handy a piece of waste knitting, so that I need not actually cast on, but can just pick up stitches), knit until the collar is long enough, put the collar stitches on to waste yarn, and continue on the edging stitches only.

(*d*) Some patterns give instructions for a collar (in rib or stitch pattern) where the whole collar is knitted in one stitch, then cast off and sewn to the neck edge. It is not easy to make a good job of attaching a collar in this way. On a double bed machine I like to finish with a few rows of tubular knitting, and then I sandwich the neck edge between the two layers of stocking stitch. With single bed work, it is sometimes an advantage to finish with a few rows of stocking stitch — decide each case on its merits.

(*e*) Knitters are often scared of shawl collars. Unless they are following a pattern exactly, and using the recommended yarn, they are worried about how to make sure — when the collar and band is knitted in one long strip — the centre back will be exactly at the centre back of the garment, so that the collar will start to curve outwards at exactly the same place on each side. In theory you should be able to get this right by carefully measuring tension — but in practice (especially in a rib) this is quite difficult: a very small difference can spoil the appearance of the garment. I knit such collars in two halves — starting at centre back with waste yarn. I do the button band first. When I have pinned this into position, I can see how many rows to unravel (I always knit longer than I need, because it is much easier to unravel a few rows than to put the band back on to the machine and knit extra rows) and where the buttonholes should come. When I have knitted both halves, I graft the centre back stitches together, making an invisible join. If the collar and band are knitted in a stitch pattern which makes grafting difficult, then I start at the centre back with a normal closed-edge cast-on and sew centre back seam — but it is usually possible to make shawl collars in either stocking stitch or simple rib, so that they can be grafted.

(*f*) Stocking stitch collars can be knitted tubular if you have a double bed machine or a ribbing attachment. I like to do a row of every-needle rib a few rows before completing a tubular collar — this seals the two halves together and in my view makes the collar 'sit' better. On a single bed machine, if after I have joined the short edges of the collar I feel that it does not look as good as it should, I have sometimes worked a row of zig-zag machine stitching across it (just where the ribbing would have come) and found that this improved it. Sometimes when a collar (tubular or stocking stitch) refuses to 'go right' I have cured it by undoing and re-knitting with the stitch size for the underneath of the collar slightly smaller than for the top. These small points are not always mentioned in machine knitting patterns, so it is worth while doing a little experimenting for yourself. A well fitting collar really 'lifts' knitwear.

(*g*) Sometimes it is an advantage to interface tubular or stocking stitch collars with interfacing such as Vilene (see Chapter Sixteen).

Pockets

It is simple to knit either a patch or a set-in pocket, by following the instructions in your knitting pattern (or instruction book). But what used to defeat me was how to attach the patch pocket to the main garment, or how to finish the top of the set-in pocket, in a professional-looking way.

Lots of practice, and experimenting, have taught me to do both jobs neatly. I sometimes find I can get better results by using a matching sewing thread (Drima or Gutermann's) instead of the yarn. Sometimes a patch pocket looks good saddle stitched, in a darker tone, usually to match stripes or fair isle on another part of the garment.

Nowadays I do not sew patch pockets on the garment. I knit the front first, decide where I want the pocket to be, turn the front of the garment round (so that the right side is facing the machine) with the hem downwards, and pick up the required number of stitches at the point where I want the bottom of the pocket to be. I then knit the pocket, *picking up the stitches on the garment* (each side of the pocket) as I go. When the pocket is as deep as I want, I knit one row on a loose tension (for the fold line of the pocket top) decrease one stitch each side of the pocket (this is to make it easier to tuck the flap inside and stitch into position) and knit the inside of the hem. I cast off or strip off and either slip stitch into position or fix with adhesive hemming web.

If I want to make a set-in pocket, I sometimes cheat by making only a very narrow pocket top. I recently made a cardigan in Jaeger Spiral Spun, which is a thick soft wool, and I rather dreaded neatening the pocket top. But I made the welt by knitting 2 rows at T. 9, 1 row at T. 10, 2 rows at T. 9. I made a doubled edge, and it looked good without any sewing up. That cardigan has had some quite hard wear, and been washed a number of times: the pocket top still looks excellent (better than the deeper hem that is more usual).

Some knitters knit the pocket lining with — say — 36 stitches, but they knit the pocket top (on the main part of the garment) with only 34. This means that when they put the pocket lining stitches on the empty needles that have just knitted the pocket top, they will have two extra stitches — which means there will be two stitches on one needle at each end of the pocket opening. This helps to fill in the nasty little 'crack' that sometimes, otherwise, appears at the edge of the pocket top. You can cheat by binding the garment with bought braid. Then you can trim the pocket tops with this, extending it slightly each side of the pocket to hide an imperfect join.

Remember that however good your work, knitting is essentially a stretch fabric — if people constantly push their hands into knitted pockets, or cram them with car keys and dog leads and loose change, then they will stretch. If you feel this is likely to happen, you can interface and line pockets — it takes time, but can be worth while with determined pocket-wreckers.

One or two other things I have learned about pockets:

If you knit pocket lining before the front of the garment, and decide where the bottom of the pocket lining is to be attached to the garment, you can put the stitches from the first row of lining on to the stitches for the main garment (at the appropriate place in the row), knit them together, and continue knitting on main garment only. Knit the same number of rows as you knitted for the pocket lining. Knit pocket top. Cast (or strip) off. Lift stitches from last row of pocket lining on to the empty needles and continue knitting right across garment. This lining does not have to be sewn down at the bottom — only down the sides.

Some knitters prefer loose pocket linings (say these 'bag' less). Knit to where you want the pocket top to start, put all needles into holding position except those needed for the pocket top. Knit top (welt) of pocket, make a hem (by picking up stitches so that there are two stitches on every needle across the pocket top), then knit twice the depth needed for the pocket. Put needles from holding position back into work, continue knitting front of garment. This pocket lining is not stitched to the garment — only sewn down the side seams: it forms a loose bag.

The 'Buttonhole Pocket' is one of the quickest and easiest, and since I tried it, some years ago, I have used it more than any other pocket. Knit the front of the garment, but when you come to the point where you would like the pocket opening to be knitted in a contrast thread (casting-on cord, or anything fine and strong, in a contrast colour) over all the needles you want for your pocket. You do this exactly as if you were making a giant buttonhole. Continue knitting. When the front is finished you pick up (on the machine) the stitches for the welt, and knit this. You can either cast or strip off and sew down later, or you can make a hem and cast off. Then turn the garment the other way up, pick up stitches for the pocket lining, and knit this. The pocket lining has to be sewn down at the bottom and sides. I find these pockets a time-saver, and very satisfactory.

Neckbands

are the Waterloo of many knitters. Sometimes the pattern writers don't help . . . There are still patterns around that tell you to knit the neckband all at the same stitch size, and sometimes these bands do not fit well. It is quite easy to do your own shaping-by-tension, and get a much better fitting band: if you are told to knit 30 rows, all at the same stitch size, knit 5 rows at recommended size, 5 rows one point (not one whole size) smaller, 10 rows 2 points smaller, 5 rows one point larger, 5 rows one point larger (that is, the same stitch size as the first rows). To make this absolutely clear, let us say that the stitch size given for the neckband is 4, and the number of rows 30. Knit 5 rows at T. 4 — 5 rows at T. 3.. (three and two dots — or if your machine is marked in quarters, then three and three quarters) — 10 rows at T. 3. (three and one dot) — 5 rows at T. 3.. and 5 rows at T. 4.

But it is the finishing that so many knitters make such a poor job of. (I have talked about this in Chapter Eight, but I cannot over-stress the importance of this point.) *Many* knitters — not just the odd few — come to grief here. And I think it is not so much lack of instruction as a wrong attitude.

Far too many knitters do not grasp the fact that a lot of *really expensive luxury knitwear*, sold at very high prices in tip-top stores, *is made on the ordinary home knitting machine*. If you look in the windows of some of the best shops you can actually see this for yourselves: visiting friends in the Midlands I looked in the window of a man's outfitters. A brown polo necked sweater was on display — price tag £12.75 — with a fair isle design that I have used at least a dozen times (punch card M 21, set 1002 on my Knitmaster 323). The polo neck was knitted in a mock rib, finished with a few rows of stocking stitch, turned to the right side and backstitched (just as I have described). It was a beautiful garment, deserving a place in a very high-class shop window. *You and I can do work as good as this.* It is only accepting second best that holds knitters back.

Hems

---

can also bring problems. They can be:

(*a*) Too wide for the rest of the garment. This usually means you have not reduced the stitch size sufficiently. TRY IT OUT is the golden rule for all knitting problems (and you can do this *quickly* with machine knitting), but as a general guide, if I am using stitch size 7 for a garment, I would knit the inside of the hem with stitch size 5 and the outside with stitch size 6. But when I do my tension square, I always go on knitting for a few more inches and then make a hem — just as I mean to make it on the garment. Then I can see how it will look and alter the stitch size(s) if necessary.

Sometimes the hem itself is satisfactory, but there is a tendency to stand out where the joining row has been knitted. I get a better effect, often, by knitting this row at a larger tension. Again, try this out on your tension square.

Sometimes, in spite of careful knitting and adjusting the stitch sizes, there is still a 'fluting out' problem which spoils the look of the garment. This happens more often with synthetics than with wool. I make a closed edge cast-on, knit the hem (but don't close it), continue knitting and then slip stitch hem into position when the garment is finished. If the problem arises with pure wool, I fix the hem with iron-on hemming web, which is not only quicker than sewing but gives a nice firmness to the hem. But most synthetics won't take the heat and steam necessary for this.

I am getting more and more in favour of the hem that is stitched (or stuck) into position and less and less in favour of the hem that is knitted in. I know some knitters will disagree with me — and most machine knitting patterns still tell us to pick up the stitches to close the hem — but it seems to me that, especially with synthetics, knitted-in hems can be the weak spot in otherwise beautiful knitting. Only last week I attended a fashion show run by a large knitting machine centre. The garments were delightful — such good colours, clever designs (many of them original) and generally high standard. But even here, some of the hems — as the models walked across the stage — looked pulled in, or uneven. It was the only fault I spotted, throughout a wonderful show, and I couldn't help thinking that stitching — or sticking — those hems would have been an improvement.

(*b*) Even if you have a double bed machine or a ribbing attachment, it is not always a good idea to knit hems tubular. They may 'flute' out.

(*c*) The row of knitting where the stitches have been picked up may look clumsy, in some yarns. Try casting on over alternate needles — you can push the remaining needles up into working position in the second row. This means that only half the needles will have two stitches on them, instead of every needle. If the whole hem looks bulky (as it can do in thick yarn) knit the inside of the hem either with a finer matching yarn, or with the same yarn but on every other needle.

(*d*) Sometimes — especially with synthetics — a hem may stretch after it has been washed several times. Insert a piece of flat strong elastic through the hem, catching it at the side seams for a sweater, at the front bands for a jacket.

(*e*) Good knitting patterns usually give a curved hem for dresses, skirts etc, but some knitters ignore this (think it difficult or unnecessary) and knit straight — ending up with an ugly dip each side of the bottom of the skirt. Hem shaping is very simple (it is only using the holding position to knit a few less rows on the edge stitches than on the centre stitches, so that the length measured down the centre of the skirt — which is straight — shall be the same as the length measured down the side seams — which are sloped). Next time you use a pattern that gives a curved hem, read it through carefully; it sometimes looks complicated because a number of sizes are given in brackets, but if you sort out your size only you will see how simple it is. It can make a great difference to your skirt hems.

(*f*) Beginners are sometimes puzzled by the 'loose tension' row. This is only to give a nice flat fold line. Try this: with waste yarn knit a few rows, knit one row on a much looser tension — about three whole sizes — then go back to the main tension, knit a few more rows and strip off. You will see that where you have knitted the loose row there is a natural fold — it looks almost as if the fabric had been pressed.

(*g*) Another worry is: if I knit the inside of a hem on a smaller stitch size than the outside, does this mean I should knit the same number of rows before and after the loose row, or should I knit one row fewer on the outside, to make up for the tighter tension on the inside? I don't know of a hard and fast rule, that will apply every time, but in practice if I am using a very fine yarn I knit the same number of rows before and after the loose row (because one row of fine knitting does not make any appreciable difference to length). If I am using a thick yarn, I sometimes find it advisable to knit one row fewer for the outside of the hem. But — as I have said — I try out my hems when doing my tension squares, so I can decide this before starting the garment. This problem does not arise if you stitch or stick your hem.

Cuffs

---

are usually easy to follow from patterns — except that in some older patterns you may be told to cast on — say — 50 stitches, then remove the work from the machine, push up 75 needles, replace the stitches on to these needles, increasing evenly . . . This is most irritating to do, so don't do it.

Ignore the instructions for this cuff. Using waste yarn, cast on for the sleeve (as if the cuff didn't exist). When you have knitted the sleeve, push up the number of needles required for the cuff (in your pattern) and replace the sleeve stitches on to these needles *decreasing* evenly all the way across. This is very much easier than increasing.

Or you can knit the sleeve from the top downwards, if you prefer.

If it is a wide sleeve, gathered into a cuff, there may be a big difference between the number of stitches on the sleeve and the number required for a cuff. If you have 100 stitches on the sleeve, and 50 for the cuff it is simple — you put two stitches on every needle. But it does not always work out as easily as that. Say you have 120 stitches for the sleeve, and 50 for the cuff — 50 does not go evenly into 120, so break it down into small sections: you need to put 12 stitches on to 5 needles. This means two stitches on every needle, with 2 over. Try this out:

1st needle	2 stitches	
2nd ,,	2 ,,	
3rd ,,	3 ,,	
4th ,,	2 ,,	
5th ,,	3 ,,	
Total 5 needles	12 stitches	Repeat all the way along.

Cardigan Bands

These are as important as the neckline, from the point of view of giving your garment a professional appearance, and much of what was said about neckbands applies to front (and armhole) bands. But front bands are much easier, because the fronts of a garment are straight, or slightly sloped, and not curved like a neckline. It is much easier to pick up smoothly so that no holes show.

For lengthwise bands, knitted in stocking stitch, the perfect finish is mattress stitch. This takes time, and though it is well worth it for top quality garments in expensive yarns, I now very often machine stitch bands to fronts (I catch down the inside by hand, but this can be done quickly). Make sure the band does not twist as you machine: careful pinning ought to take care of this, but if you run into trouble, try putting in coloured markers, as you knit — say every 50 rows. You can match these up as you pin and stitch.

Many knitters say it is not possible to machine-stitch ribbed bands on to fronts; until recently I agreed with them. But a clever knitter I often work with started to experiment and her results were so good that I adopted this way too. We find it helps to have one extra stitch at one edge (this makes a little channel to machine stitch along). The work must be well and carefully done — otherwise it looks terrible. Again, it is a matter of taking a little time, and a lot of determination, and *practising* until you are good at it. If you can't do a really good job, stick to hand-sewing (I like a flat 'weaving' stitch).

Length

(especially in dresses, skirts and trousers) often worries knitters, even when they are scrupulous about making and measuring a tension square. It is not always easy to decide the exact length needed until the garment is tried on (dressmakers adjust at this stage). If you are unsure of the finished length, then leave the hem loose — you can stitch or stick (with hemming web) after trying on. Some knitters are put off using hemming web (adhesive) because they think they will not be able to remove this if they make a mistake, or want to alter a hemline. But in most cases it can be removed — simply by ironing again and peeling off while it is still warm. Try this out on a small piece of waste knitting.

If you leave the hem open, to adjust after trying on, you should omit the loose tension row. It is often an advantage to knit skirts and trousers from the waist downwards (easier to adjust length).

Openings

are another worry to knitters. Patterns often tell us to finish an opening (before inserting a zip, or making button loops) with a row of double crochet, but on adult garments this can look very home-made, unless done by an expert. I face openings whenever I can. If the garment is knitted in a stitch pattern, I usually do this by picking up stitches along the opening. If it is in stocking stitch, then I knit it all in one: after dividing for the opening I decide how many stitches I want for the facing (say 10).

Put 10 stitches from the holding position needles (for the other half of the front or back) on to waste yarn and use these ten empty needles for the facing. It helps to have ready a piece of knitting 10 stitches wide and about 2″ (10 cm) deep, in the yarn you are using for the garment. Place these stitches on to the empty needles, and you can continue without casting-on. The extra depth of 2″ (10 cm) also means you will have a neater finish to the opening — the two pieces of facing can be folded back and invisibly joined. You now knit as pattern, but when you start to shape the neck, remember you will have to cast off the ten stitches for the facing, as well as the first block of stitches you cast off for the neck shaping. I say 'cast off' but of course you can put these stitches on to waste yarn. When the garment is finished they will be hidden by neckband or collar.

Press carefully — according to the yarn you are using — and you should now have a neat, faced opening. Insert a zip — I like to do this by hand. I use a matching thread and try to sew in between two rows of (knitted) stitches, so that it is almost invisible. Just above the base of the opening I make a firm tailor's tack, so that the zip cannot go too far, and to prevent strain on the opening, I turn the garment inside out and make another strong tailor's tack to hold the zip tapes together just above the zip stop.

Buttonholes

worry a good many knitters, even though instruction books tell — and show — how these should be done.

It is largely a matter of practice. I made a mess of buttonholes until I faced up to this, made a load of knitted bands, marked out buttonholes with contrast thread, and sat down determinedly and practised grafting the stitches (exactly as it says in the instruction book). After a time I could do a neat buttonhole — but it still needs care and patience.

For those who simply haven't the time (because they are turning out masses of cheap garments) or who have some difficulty in using their hands, or whose sight is not good — as well as for those who simply want to take a short cut — here are a few suggestions:

(*1*) Just now the fashion is for tie fastenings — take advantage of it. You can make ties with cord knitting, with a narrow strip of ribbing, with crochet or by twisting or plaiting. You can add tiny toggles or balls, or make bobbles.

(*2*) You can cheat by leaving gaps between edge of garment and band, and using these gaps as buttonholes.

(*3*) You can take advantage of the attractive button-type snap fasteners now on sale — but try these out on a spare piece of knitting. Not all yarns are tough enough to take them.

(*4*) Look round the haberdashery departments and consider all the dressmaking aids — toggles, fancy hooks and eyes, frog fastenings, buckles etc.

(*5*) You can (sometimes — with luck!) make buttonholes on the sewing machine. Some experienced knitters say it cannot be done — but others do it quite well. One expert knitter said to me: "It's an adventure. Sometimes it works splendidly — sometimes it doesn't. You just have to try it out."

Perivale-Gutermann Limited (the well known makers of sewing threads, whose 100% polyester sewing thread is a great help to those who like to make up their knitting on a sewing machine) took the trouble to do a number of tests for me, and this is a summary of their advice:

(*1*) It is vital to try the buttonhole on a scrap of spare knitting first. A

Carol Williams of Metropolitan Sewing Machine Co. of Bournemouth — who does so much to help machine knitters — made this beautiful flowing gown in nylon-tricel for £2.20. She knitted straight pieces of material, and used the cut-and-sew method (though she assures me she is no dressmaker). Even the braid (very expensive to buy nowadays) is knitted.

trial like this enables you to see how wide the zig-zag should be (so that there is enough cover), to check the colour of the sewing thread against the fabric (it will look different in buttonhole form); to check the length of buttonhole required (buy your buttons first) and count the number of stitches required to give this length. Only when you have done all this should you start on the buttonholes on the garment.

(*2*) Mark the length of the buttonholes and make sure both sides are the same length.

(*3*) Stitch the first side, and finish with the needle in the work in the right-hand stroke of the zig-zag.

(*4*) Turn the work and stitch the second leg of the buttonhole (making sure it is the same length as the first) and leaving a small space between the two sides (legs) so that the stitches will not be cut when you cut open the buttonhole.

(*5*) Do all the buttonholes required to this stage before changing stitch width.

(*6*) Set the throw of the needle bar wide enough to cover the outside edges of both sides of the buttonhole.

(*7*) Set the stitch density to 0.

(*8*) Bar-tack all the buttonholes making sure that the stitches at each end of the buttonholes are covered.

(*9*) Cut the hole *carefully*. If by some misfortune you cut the stitches of the sides of the buttonhole, carefully unpick the bar tack and remake the buttonhole over the existing stitches. *Do not try to unpick them.* Then re-do the bar tack.

(*10*) If necessary, reduce the pressure on the presser foot to eliminate differential feeding (one layer of fabric moving more quickly or more slowly than the other).

You will see that no mention is made of using an automatic buttonholer — where it is not necessary to turn the work. This is because the machinists doing the testing found that — for machine knitted fabrics — they seemed to get better results by stitching always in a forward direction (which means that you must turn the work).

But remember our knitter who said it was 'an adventure . . .' When you do your trial buttonhole — on a spare piece of knitting — by all means try out your automatic buttonholer if you have one. It may be that your fabric will be firm enough, or your machine a particularly good one, and you will achieve good results. If not, then try out the way suggested above — which is the result of a good many patient tests.

I would just like to add that I always get better results when I reinforce the knitted fabric in some way — either with a piece of fine linen or cotton, or iron-on interfacing. Buttonholes should be vertical.

15
Making Money with your Knitting Machine

I *know* it is possible to make money with a knitting machine. This is not an advertising gimmick, but sober fact.

I know because I have a bulging file of letters from knitters, telling me about it. "I made the money to pay for our holiday . . ."; "I earn around £10 a week . . ."; "I've earned enough to buy a ribbing attachment . . ."; "My knitting has paid to have the loft converted . . ."; "I earn £25 to £30 a week . . .". One knitter asked a small shop to display a sample garment — "and the orders rolled in"; another took a pattern book to work, to browse through in her lunch hour — "and within an hour I had £40 worth of orders"; another put up a notice and price list "and the result was overwhelming".

And I know because I do it myself. I am a full time writer, and have a home, so I cannot knit regularly. But I am deeply involved with one or two charities, cannot afford to give them as much as I should like, and so run a tiny cottage industry, based on machine knitting. I make a very fair profit which is shared between various good causes.

But let's be realistic. Your knitting machine is not a gadget where you push a ball of wool in at one end, and pound notes pour out at the other.

Earning money in your own home — while still caring for your family and keeping your house clean — is not usually the way to make a fortune. A few people, with special gifts — the artist, the sculptor, the potter — may make quite large sums. At the other end of the scale, some homework is so poorly paid, involves so much mess and upheaval and is so boring and tedious that unless you are desperate for a few extra pounds it is not worth while.

Between these extremes — and pretty near the top, in my view — comes machine knitting.

You may not earn as much as a shorthand-typist or a skilled factory worker. But you'll be in your own cosy home, while they are queuing at the bus stop in the cold rain. You can take the morning off and walk the dog through the park (as long as you make up the time afterwards).

You'll be handling lovely yarns, and doing something you enjoy, while they are thumping out invoices or pushing buttons. You won't get paid for holidays — but you can take those holidays when you like. You'll be there when your husband and children come home, or when one of them is ill. You'll find yourself getting better and better at your craft, which means your life will be full of interest. Your work will speed up, which means your earnings should increase with your skill. Like many knitters, you'll probably get to the stage where you have more orders than you can manage, and then you have the choice: either accept only those orders that pay well, and that you like doing, or find some help and start your own small business — which in time could become a large business. Many flourishing ventures started with just one person and a knitting machine.

How to Make a Start

Don't try to sell your knitwear until it is good. You may find an odd neighbour who will take second-rate work — but people will get to know where it came from and soon you'll have a reputation as the woman who makes nasty sweaters! A bad reputation is hard to live down, so much better wait until you can make garments that people admire — then they'll talk about them and do your advertising for you. (But this does not mean you cannot start small. Some knitters start with just one item — like scarves, or school sweaters. But they must be *excellent* scarves or school sweaters.)

Even when your work is good, you need to tell the world about it. Sometimes the best way to do this is just to wear it — or let other people wear it. One knitter told me she had knitted a jacket for her granddaughter, who wore it to work, and forty of her colleagues begged 'Gran' to knit for them, too. If this doesn't work for you, put a notice in a local shop window, or local paper, or approach suitable shops, or hold a knitting party . . .

But if you do this, remember that there are now so many 'selling parties' that most women are sick and tired of them. So make it clear in your invitation that this is a pre-view only — you are not selling anything, only showing people the sort of thing you can do. If this is made clear, people will accept the invitation more willingly (they won't be embarrassed if they don't want to buy) and if they like your knitwear they can — and will — get in touch with you again.

You may find an 'agent' — perhaps a friend who works in a large firm, or school, or hospital — anywhere where she comes in contact with plenty of people. Even if she is a close friend, it is better for both of you to be businesslike. Keep records of everything she takes away, everything she brings back unsold, all the money she pays you. Pay her a commission, and any agreed out-of-pocket expenses (such as fares or petrol). Make sure that everything you give her is of saleable quality, packed in a nice clean plastic bag, clearly marked with price, size, type of yarn used (and washing or pressing instructions if necessary).

Or you may like to work through a shop (or shops). Find the sort of shop you like the look of — and go and ask if they are interested. If the first one refuses, find another . . . sooner or later someone is going to welcome the idea. Some shops buy outright, others want goods on sale-or-return. In this case I suggest a short trial run — you should make sure that you will get back unsold goods in as-new condition.

Lately I have heard of several knitters (sometimes groups of knitters) who are renting stalls in their local market, and seem to be doing well.

You may decide you will work only to order. This is not as interesting or creative as building up your own stock — you may be asked to knit some very dull things. It also means you will be asked to knit some 'awkward' shapes and sizes (the Knit Radar is a great help here). But it does mean you will not be left with unsold goods on your hands (ask for a deposit, when the order is placed, sufficient to cover cost of yarn). If you are starting small, and can't afford to take even small risks, this could be the right way to begin.

You can also look for outwork (watch the advertisements in the local paper) which usually pays less than taking orders or selling your own goods, but is also less demanding.

And you can — if you wish — specialise: children's clothes, club sweaters, large sizes, difficult figures, evening wear, wedding dresses.

How Much Should You Charge?

Once upon a time knitters usually charged by the ounce. Now more and more of them are charging by the hour, basing the figure on what is currently being earned by other skilled workers (e.g. dressmakers). The local employment department may be able to advise. But this too has its drawbacks — if you are a quick worker, it is a good bargain for the customer; if you are slow you may price yourself out of the market.

Some successful knitters simply look around — in the better shops if they are producing top quality knitwear, in chain stores and mail order ads if they are making 'run of the mill' garments — and fix their prices slightly below shop prices, remembering that shops have to pay wages, rent, rates, VAT and a host of other expenses, while the home knitter usually has to pay only for materials (including buttons, zips, sewing threads etc), possibly some heat in her workroom and any expenses incurred in posting or delivering orders. To charge in this way your work *must be good*. It must be made in good quality yarn, correctly knitted and carefully finished, and you must be as fair to your customers as a reputable shop would be — that is, if there is legitimate cause for complaint you must be willing to replace or refund.

On the other hand, if you are outstandingly good, and if you produce original designs, made to measure, then you would be justified in asking more than the customer would pay for 'off the peg' knitwear.

Everything has to be done with flexibility and common sense. Play sweaters won't sell for as much as evening tops — even though they take as long to make; you can't charge as much in a depressed area as you can in a thriving one . . . You will quickly learn what is best, from your point of view, and try to concentrate on the garments that make the most money for you.

You Need Time

if you are going to earn money by knitting. Unless you already have a good deal of spare time, that you want to fill, this may mean some reorganisation, and this should be done before you take on any knitting commitments. Otherwise you will start off worried and rushed — and this lowers efficiency and spoils the fun of a new venture.

If you are knitting to help the family budget, then the family should join in. See if some of them can take on some of your chores. It makes sense to use some of your earnings to buy yourself time — an automatic washing machine, a deep freeze, a dishwasher — any of these will save you time which you can use for more knitting. If you do well, it may be a good idea to try to get paid help — either in the house, or another knitter, or someone who does the pressing and making up while you knit.

You Must Keep Records

From the word go, you should keep records of:-

(*a*) All orders taken (with details of pattern, measurements, colour, customer's name and address, delivery date etc). Note down what yarn you use, and how much, what stitch size, any alterations to printed pattern. And of course you will have your tension note book — or box of labelled tension squares.
(*b*) Every penny you spend on yarn, trimmings etc.
Other expenses, such as petrol if you have to deliver goods (or fares).
Special 'knitting' expenses, like extra heating for the room where you work.
Commission paid to anyone who sells for you.
Every penny you receive in payment.

You need (*a*) because this information will help you to work efficiently. You need (*b*) because without this information you may not pay tax which is due (and so find yourself in trouble) or pay more tax than you need have paid (because you did not keep any record of expenses).

In the United Kingdom there is no need for the small knitter to panic at the thought of tax. For your own peace of mind you should *declare* your earnings, but this does not mean you will have to pay tax on them (if they are small). There are all sorts of concessions — for married women, for people on low incomes, for people over sixty . . . As long as your knitting is just a profitable hobby, bringing you in up to £12 a week (and you are not in other paid employment) it may well be that neither you nor your husband will have to pay tax on your knitting earnings — and £12 a week, even in these days of inflation, is a nice addition to the family budget. But you should check with your local tax office. They are usually helpful to those who obviously want to be straight and keep their affairs in good order.

And whatever your age or income, you are entitled to deduct legitimate expenses from your earnings. For instance, if you paid £2.00 for the wool for a sweater, plus 20p for buttons, plus 15p fare to deliver it, and you sell it for £5.00, then you pay tax (*if any*) on £2.65 and not on £5.00. This clearly shows how important it is to keep a record of your expenses. (Keep receipts, too, wherever possible). When you reach the stage of having to pay tax on your earnings, you may be able to claim a proportion of household expenses (rent, rates, heating, lighting etc). If you own your own home, you should take advice before applying for this — it could affect your capital gains tax position. Also if you live in council-owned property, there may be restrictions on earning at home. Check carefully.

If you decide to go into business — even if you run that business from home — you may need more advice than the tax office will have time to give you, and you should consult an accountant.

Your Bank manager can probably recommend a local accountant — perhaps a retired man who still does some work. Ask if — for a fee — you can go and have a chat with him. Take a list of the questions you want to ask (this saves his time and your money). If you find him helpful and reasonable, you then have someone you can turn to for advice in the future.

A competent accountant will not charge the earth. He (more than anyone!) knows how much you can afford. But he will do — quickly and correctly — what it may take you ages to do (and then you may make mistakes) leaving you free to knit, design, and sell.

In the United Kingdom another source of help for freelance earners, or anyone else with tax problems, is *The Income Tax Payers' Society*. Membership costs only a few pounds a year and entitles you to tax advice.

Wherever you seek advice, you must be able to give the full facts — what you have spent, and what you have earned, with receipts if possible for all expenditure. Without this information the best accountant in the world cannot do a good job for you.

Suppose you have tried — hard — to make money with your knitting machine, and failed? What can be done?

First find the reason — then try to deal with it.

Is Your Work Good Enough To Sell?

Even for the very tiny cottage industry I run, I have had so much poor work sent to me that I feel sure this is the major reason for failure to earn. I *wanted* to ask those knitters to work with me, but I couldn't because I knew their work would not sell. Usually the knitting was fine, but the making up was clumsy and amateurish. This can be cured — with practice and determination. Go back to your instruction book, go back to Chapters Seven, Eight, Nine, Fourteen. Use up all your oddments of yarn, and keep trying until you can do a really good job. Most of all, keep looking at top quality knitwear — in the shops, in fashion magazines — and make up your mind to reach the same standard.

Are You Getting The Right Publicity?

To earn money with your machine, you must either advertise (directly or

GET A GOOD IDEA (and a knitting machine) and you can vary it in so many ways. Full-length, incorporating a glitter yarn, this is an evening dress to be proud of (it's warm, too, without being grannified). Shorter, in a cotton or synthetic, it's a useful button-through for summer days. And in something cosy (like pure wool, wool mixture or some of the softer synthetics) and with longer sleeves, it's a housecoat (you choose the length).

indirectly) or you must find a shop or an agent to sell for you. This seems too obvious to mention, but I actually know of knitters who have sat at home, disappointed that they did not get orders or sell the goods they had made, doing nothing to tell the world what they had to offer.

Are You Charging Too Much?

Even if your work is really good, prices must be realistic. You may (I hope you will) one day make a real name for yourself in the fashion world — and then you can charge ridiculous prices. But most knitters have to start fairly cautiously. If your goods are dearer *than comparable goods* from other sources, this could be the reason for failure.

Are You Charging Too Little?

If so, you are probably selling all you can make, but earning very little.

Keep your eye on shop prices — be realistic. Most knitters come across a few (fortunately usually a very few) customers who expect them to work for next to nothing. If you want to help someone who is really hard up, by keeping your prices low for her — fine. But don't let people sponge on you. One knitter was actually told "Oh, I don't want anything if you are going to charge for the knitting. I thought if I paid for the wool that would be enough." (I wonder if she expected the window cleaner to clean the windows for nothing — if she gave him the water?) Have nothing to do with customers like this (there are plenty of nice ones around). Charge a fair price for your work, and stick to it.

Are You In A Rut?

Some knitters produce nice work, but it is all 'much of a muchness'. Chain stores sell good knitwear, at reasonable prices — and they have huge stocks to choose from. You can't compete with them — they are bigger than you are — so aim at being different. Successful knitters have often developed some lines of their own — extra-colourful fair isle, or embroidered knitting, or extra-large sizes, or lace work, or patchwork knitting, or club or school colours, or . . . or . . . There's a wide choice.

Have You Looked Far Enough Afield?

I have had several letters from knitters who tried everything — and they assure me their work was good — but couldn't get started. Then — either through moving their home, or just spending a day in a neighbouring town and approaching shops there — their luck has changed. It could be that some districts are not good hunting grounds.

Are You So Slow That Your Earnings Are Low?

We are all slow when we first begin. But with practice we speed up. Keep knitting, make use of all the time-savers you can find — see Chapters Seven, Nine, Fourteen, Sixteen. I am sure it now takes me about half as long to knit a garment as it did when I was a beginner. That's how it will be for you, too.

16
Help for Machine Knitters

The more you use your knitting machine, the more you will realise that it is not just a hotted-up pair of knitting needles, but a marvellous piece of equipment for producing clothes (and furnishings) in many different ways, and that nearly everything that helps the dressmaker can also help and interest the machine knitter. I am surprised how few machine knitters take advantage of all the expertise there is around, and should like to mention some of the things I find really useful.

Vilene Interfacings

enable many amateur dressmakers to achieve professional looking results: in my view they are just as helpful to machine knitters.

Any knitter who is keen to branch out and get away from the traditional cardigan-and-sweater image of knitting should look carefully at Vilene products and consider what they can do for her knitting. You can see these products in good shops or stores that sell dressmaking fabrics, paper patterns etc — and the leaflet *How to choose and use Vilene* should also be available. In case of difficulty, write to Vilene. They can advise you of your nearest stockist and they are always sympathetic to problems in dressmaking and machine knitting.

You will find there is a wide range of interfacings — some iron-on, some to be sewn in — all capable of enormously improving the appearance of a garment, all having their special uses. Three products that I find particularly helpful, with machine knitting, are:

Superdrape, an interfacing especially designed for knitwear; it makes it possible to give body and firmness to a piece of knitting without making it rigid and non-stretch (which would spoil its special quality).

Wundaweb — I like this for hems and pocket tops.

Bondaweb — this is for fusing two pieces of material together and I like it for applying motifs to otherwise plain garments. For the knitter with only a simple machine, who wants to make something eye-catching, this is one of the most interesting ways.

Remember: iron-on interfacings need heat: you must test carefully before using them on synthetics and you must always follow the maker's instructions exactly.

Floppy collars or pocket tops, limp cuffs, facings that won't lie flat, belts that roll over or twist — this is the sort of problem that Vilene products can so often help a knitter with. In fact whenever I want to get a really professional finish — especially on light weight garments — I think of Vilene, and very often it is the right answer.

Buttons

do not have to be the boring round plastic things that appear on so many knitted garments. It is worth while to look through the wide selection that some of the bigger stores, or specialist shops, have. But remember that a too-heavy button (which is fine on woven fabric) may pull knitting out of shape.

Really nice buttons are expensive, so you can try covering your own. Neweys have some good button moulds — I like Trims nylon buttons and *Clear Top* buttons (look on your haberdashery counter). To use these, your knitted fabric must be firm but not bulky. If you are using several strands of coned synthetics, you may find you make a better button-covering material with fewer strands than you used for the garment, and a finer tension.

Or you can have buttons and buckles covered professionally. A number of firms do this work well — especially Harlequin, who also cover belts (send s.a.e. for their leaflet).

This firm also stock muslin for pressing cloths and in my view this is much better than any other material. I value my muslin pressing cloth and should not like to work without it.

You can also crochet buttons: simply start with 4 chain, join into a ring, then work double crochet into the ring, increasing until you have the desired size, then decreasing again. If you like, you can give the button a rounder shape by working one or two rows without either increasing or decreasing. It is very easy to see what shape your button is taking, and adjust as you work. You can stuff these with oddments of matching wool, then they'll wash and dry exactly as the garment. Or if you prefer, you can insert a suitable button mould. Or you can blanket stitch, or work double crochet, over a plastic ring and then darn in the centre. You can also crochet a tight, firm circle, of suitable size, and use this flat. This is good for bed jackets or baby clothes, where hard buttons could be painful if leaned against.

Buttonholes

are anathema to many knitters (see Chapter Fourteen) so again look on the haberdashery counter and in the trimmings department — there are various ways of getting out of the job of making buttonholes.

Neweys come to the rescue again with their *Poppa Fasteners* and *Buttonsnaps*. Remember: not all knitted fabrics can take this type of fastening. *Try it out first.* This firm also makes fur hooks — if you are using oddments of fur fabric to trim a jacket, housecoat, etc, these could be the answer to the fastening problem.

Before we leave this very useful firm, I'd like to tell you about their loose cover pins (the two-pronged kind — not the 'corkscrew' kind) — which are really for soft furnishing, but are splendid for pinning your knitting in position on the pressing board. Much better than ordinary pins and quicker too, because you don't need so many of them. But if you prefer dressmakers' pins then you should look for Newey's *Dorcas* with coloured glass heads. It is so easy to overlook an all-metal pin — it can merge into a tweedy or Shetland yarn and be very difficult to find until you stab it into your finger. These little glass-headed pins are easy to see — and easy to pull out.

And finally, Neweys make snap fastener tape for knitted or woven cushion covers — neat, strong and easy to use.

A Roll of Sellotape

is always in my workroom. Whenever I have to push needles forward into holding position, or knit them down with long loops of contrast wool, I stick a piece of sellotape on the needle bed behind or in front of the needle butts. Then I cannot accidentally push or pull those needles back into working position before I am ready for them (and the needles holding long loops won't move and drop the loops).

I also use my sellotape for sticking short lengths of yarn beside the tension notes referring to that particular yarn. This is not so important when you are working with branded yarns — the name is sufficient — but when you are using coned yarns that you may have bought in the market or as a 'job lot' you need a piece of the actual yarn for identification.

Trimmings

If you aim to produce top-quality, original garments, take every opportunity of looking at what is available in fringes, braids, bead trimmings, fake fur edgings, bobble braid, tassels etc. Of course you can make many trimmings on your knitting machine, but there are some items, produced by specialised firms using specialised machinery, that we cannot copy. I recently saw a plain black evening dress — the only trimming was a narrow plaited gold braid — it looked superb. Look not only in the dressmakers' trimmings department, but in the furnishing trimmings too. Some of their fringes and bobbles are very suitable for ponchos etc — and often much cheaper than dressmakers' trimmings.

If you want to make your own fringe, you can do so on the machine: see your instruction book. The general idea is simple — you have a few needles in working position, then a long gap (you leave needles in non-working position, the number depending on how long you want the strands of your fringe to be), then you put a few more needles into working position. You thus knit two very narrow strips, with long threads between them. You can double the two knitted strips back on to each other, and sew one each side of the edge of the garment, or you can cut off, or unravel, the second lot of stitches.

These fringes often look quite good when working with fine coned acrylics — you should use as many strands as you can.

Another way of making fringes on your knitting machine is:

Cast on for your garment (the edge where you want a fringe) with a closed-edge cast-on. If your machine is one of those that supplies a casting-on comb, take this, make strong loops of yarn or thin string which will suspend the comb below your knitting by the required depth of the fringe. Then, with a separate ball (or balls — you can use more than one strand) of the yarn, wind this over the first needle, down and under the tooth of the comb, up and over the next needle . . . and so on. Then knit one row *very carefully*. You must use common sense (and experience) when deciding how many strands you can use at a time — there is a limit to what the machine will knit off, without being damaged. Experiment on a small piece of knitting.

If your machine does not use a casting-on comb, you can get the same effect — in fact some knitters like this way better — by holding a ruler (or the rib bar) below your row of knitting, and winding the yarn(s) round the ruler, and over the needle, for every loop. You can also do this on alternate rows and make a very interesting 'shaggy' carpet stitch — similar to that formed on double bed machines or ribbing attachments by dropping the stitches off one bed on specified rows. But when you use the ruler or casting-on comb, you can make your loops as long as you wish, within reason.

Books

I have already mentioned Mary Weaver's books (one on the Passap Duomatic and one — in two parts — on the Knitmaster 321/3 with ribbing attachment) and in my view you should not be without these books if you own one of these machines.

Your sewing machine ought to work closely with your knitting machine, if you are to achieve good, quick results; a book that I have found really helpful — in showing me all the possibilities of my sewing

Simple, but so effective — and a nice change from the usual trouser or dungaree play outfit. It is an idea that could be adapted in many ways — though these giant size motifs are a special feature of the Passap Duomatic using the JAC 40 fair isle device — and with a generous hem, the skirt could grow with the young wearer.

machine — is the *Living/Elna Sewing Book*. This is published by *Living* Magazine, and should be on sale where sewing machines are found. Although the book was written in conjunction with Elna Sewing Machines, owners of other types of swing needle machines will find a lot to interest them.

If you design, or use the cut-and-sew method, I think a good *simple* book on dressmaking is a great help, unless you are already an expert. There are some big, beautiful (and expensive) books around, but those brought out by the makers of dressmaking patterns (e.g. Simplicity or Butterick) are good and inexpensive. I also like *The Creative Art of Sewing* by Joan Fisher (Hamlyn) and anything that Ann Ladbury writes.

Some Extras

A dressmaker's dummy is handy, for jackets and cardigans.

And you must have a good pressing surface — I use an old table, with an ironing pad (old blankets and sheets) made to fit — and a good iron. I don't think you need a steam iron, as I prefer to use a damp cloth where steam is needed, but some knitters like to use steam irons. My Sunbeam can be used steam or dry — it's a lovely iron to handle and helps me enormously. I have already mentioned a muslin pressing cloth: I find this essential.

Finally, don't forget that in most areas there is some kind of machine knitting get-together, and if you can spare the time I am sure you will benefit by joining. If there isn't one in your area, what about starting one? A keen knitter I know told me: "All you need is a big teapot . . ." You can start with just two or three fellow-enthusiasts, in your living room, and go on to bigger premises if and when you need to. Machine knitting is not a cut-and-dried thing. Manufacturers keep bringing out new machines and accessories. Knitters all over the world keep having bright ideas. Meeting other knitters is the way not only to learn from them but to stimulate your own mind so that you, too, come up with brainwaves, to add to the store of experience and know-how that makes machine knitting such a fascinating (and useful, and profitable, and relaxing) hobby for those of us who are battling our way through the grim 'seventies.

Appendix

Knitting Machine Centres

Weaverknits Ltd
276-8 Main Road, Sutton-at-Hone, Dartford, Kent.
Send a large s.a.e. and ask them for their lists. They sell (mail order) 4-ply and D.K. coned acrylics in lovely colours, and these are not only very easy to knit with, but they produce beautiful garments and so help to build up your confidence, as a new knitter, and show you right from the start what wonderful results you will be able to achieve. Weaverknits also stock many spares and accessories (including the weights I mentioned in Chapter Two) and their explanatory leaflet is packed with information about the use of coned yarns — in fact it is a free knitting lesson that I wish all new knitters would study, because it would save them so much frustration and disappointment.
For the personal caller, Weaverknits have a wonderful choice of other yarns — bouclés, knops, mohairs, randoms, industrial lurex — and if you can possibly get there (it's surprisingly easy to reach) you will find it a paradise for machine knitters. There is always a display of garments that are an inspiration to new knitters. If you want to see Mary Weaver herself, you should write beforehand — she is in great demand by knitters from all parts of the country. Private lessons and repairs by arrangement.

For readers within reach of Bournemouth, another excellent centre is
Metropolitan Sewing Machine Company
130 Commercial Road, Bournemouth and 321 Ashley Road, Parkstone, Dorset.
Like Weaverknits, these people are enthusiasts. They sell knitting machines, spares, accessories, a good range of yarns (including a

repeatable 4-ply acrylic that knits up well), they have a good stock of patterns (including back issues of *Modern Knitting*) and they run a club for people who buy machines from them. This meets once a fortnight, is free, and is part social, part instructional. They have a children's knitting class, and an advisory service for people with older machines.

Another interesting place for machine knitters is the *Knitmaster Centre* at 21-25 Chiltern Street, London W.1. The machines, accessories and patterns are all Knitmaster, but the yarns — they usually have a good selection at reasonable prices — are of interest to all machine knitters. They have beautiful garments on display, and private lessons can be arranged.

Alice's Knitting and Craft Centre
225 Walworth Road, London SE17 1RL
only opened recently and is still quite small. But it is excellent for advice and tuition, as well as sales, service and yarns. 'Alice' is an exceptionally good teacher, can sort out problems for even old, out-of-date machines, and will take endless trouble for her customers or pupils.

Mail Order Firms

(Remember to send postage plus at least 10p to cover cost of shade card).

Silverknit Edwalton, Nottingham
supply luxury yarns for machine knitters, but as their yarns are economical it is luxury at a down-to-earth price. Really beautiful yarns in good colour ranges.

Cone Knit Spinning Co Prospect Mills, Wilsden, Bradford
(a new company, tied up with established spinners) have five coned yarns for machine knitters, with more planned. Prices are reasonable and I know many knitters who are delighted with the yarns.

Yorkshire Wool Co 6 Spring Gardens, Bradford.
One of the few firms offering pure wool on cones. They have a range of fifteen colours, and I have found this to knit up very well.

Foster Yarn Co (Preston) Ltd 88/96 Market Street West, Preston, Lancs.
Good range of courtelle, wool and wool/nylon on cones, from very fine to 4-ply. These yarns produce nice garments at an economical price.

Greenwood Spinning Co P.O. Box 4, Victoria Mills, Heckmondwike, W. Yorks.
have a coned Shetland with 20% nylon added, which I find very nice.

Holmfirth Wools Ltd Briggate, Windhill, Shipley, Yorkshire
stock a very good coned range, including 4-ply, D.K. and some machine-washable wool.
Direct Wool Group P.O. Box 46, Bradford
have several coned yarns for machine knitters — in attractive colours, at sensible prices. Also balled yarns which knit up well on the machine. They ask for 25p for their shade card (deducted from your first order).
MacBrigg Wool Co Main Street, Haworth, Keighley, W. Yorks BD22 8DA
have a number of coned yarns, all interesting. I like their 2-ply Shetland, 2-ply high-bulk acrylic (both knit up more like 4-ply) and their 'Sunnyside' wool/nylon.
St Johns Wools P.O. Box 55, 39 Well Street, Bradford.
Wonderful value for money, some good colours.
A mail order firm that does not (at present) have coned yarns, but is so good that I should like all knitters to know about them, is
R. S. Duncan and Co Falcon Mills, Bartle Lane, Bradford.
Very interesting shade card and high quality.

Firms That Supply Yarns in Bulk

Mailyarns 38 High Street, Syston, Leicester
have fine coned acrylics in 4 lb (1.816 kg), 6 lb (2.724 kg), 8 lb (3.632 kg) and 10 lb (4.54 kg) cartons (they have regular lines, too).
J. L. Walton and Sons (Yarns) 26 Newarke Street, Leicester
supply coned Shetland, Shetland/nylon and lambswool in 25 lb (11.35 kg) and 100 lb (45.4 kg) boxes.

With both these firms, you have to take their choice of colour (though both of them are friendly and will try to carry out your wishes if they can). Both firms quote really low prices for this kind of 'pot luck' buying, and if you are knitting for a big family, or to make garments for sale, I suggest you send s.a.e. and find out just what they have to offer.

Addresses Of Other Firms, Etc

discussed elsewhere in the book
Harlequin Ltd 258 High Street, Epping, Essex.
The Income Tax Payers' Society 1st Floor, 5 Plough Place, Fetter

Lane, London EC4A 1XN.
Living Magazine Elm House, Elm Street, London WC1X 0BP
Patons & Baldwins Ltd P.O. Box Darlington, County Durham.
Vilene Ltd P.O. Box 3, Greetland, Halifax, West Yorkshire HX4 8NJ
Mary Weaver (see *Weaverknits Ltd* at start of Appendix).

Hand Knitting Yarns

---

that I like for machine knitting:
Lee Target Motoravia — 4-ply and D.K. wears and washes well and is nice to knit.
Patons' Double Plus — pleasing texture and lovely colour range.
Patons' Bracken gives a wonderful tweedy effect when knitted in plain stocking stitch (ideal for simple machines) and because it is light weight, it goes further than some other tweed yarns.
Patons' Fiona — I think this is my favourite of all hand-knitting yarns. Wears and washes beautifully, knits easily, comes in beautiful muted shades and is warm and light.
Robin Vogue is another D.K. it is a pleasure to knit with. I have also used it for weaving, with excellent results.

In 4-ply I have made highly satisfactory garments in *Sirdar Fontein Crêpe, Jaeger Sheridan Crêpe, Patons' Purple Heather, Trident* and *Limelight* (the colours in this last yarn are exceptionally clear and brilliant).

Makers of the Knitting Machines I Use

Jones Sewing Machine Co Ltd Britannia House, 964 High Road, Finchley, London N12 9SF
(I have the 585, now superseded by the 588)
Knitmaster Limited 30-40 Elcho Street, Battersea, London SW11 4AX
(I have the 250, 323 and 326)
Passap Limited 128-9 High Street, Bordesley, Birmingham B12 0LA
(I have the Passap Duomatic)

Index